NorthStar

LISTENING AND SPEAKING

Intermediate

SECOND EDITION

Helen S. Solórzano
Jennifer P. L. Schmidt

Series Editors
Frances Boyd
Carol Numrich

Longman

NorthStar: Listening and Speaking, Intermediate, Second Edition

Pearson Education, 10 Bank Street, White Plains, NY 10606

Pronunciation consultant: Linda Lane
Development director: Penny Laporte
Project manager: Debbie Sistino
Development editors: Debbie Lazarus, Mykan White
Vice president, director of design and production: Rhea Banker
Executive managing editor: Linda Moser
Senior production editor: Kathleen Silloway
Production editor: Lynn Contrucci
Production coordinator: Melissa Leyva
Director of manufacturing: Patrice Fraccio
Senior manufacturing buyer: Dave Dickey
Photo research: Aerin Csigay
Cover design: Rhea Banker
Cover art: Detail of Wandbild aus dem Tempel der Sehnsucht\dorthin/, 1922,
    30 Mural from the temple of desire\there/ 26.7 × 37.5 cm; oil transfer
    drawing and water color on plaster-primed gauze; The Metropolitan
    Museum of Art, N.Y. The Berggruen Klee Collection, 1984. (1984.315.33)
    Photograph © 1986 The Metropolitan Museum of Art.
    © 2003 Artists Rights Society (ARS), New York / VG Bild-Kunst, Bonn
Text design: Quorum Creative Services
Text composition: ElectraGraphics, Inc.
Text font: 11/13 Sabon
Listening selections and text credits: See page 205
Text art and photo credits: See page 205

Wandbild aus dem Tempel
der Sehnsucht ↖ dorthin ↗
Paul Klee

Library of Congress Cataloging-in-Publication Data

Solórzano, Helen Sophia.
    NorthStar, Listening and Speaking, intermediate / Helen S.
Solórzano, Jennifer P.L. Schmidt—2nd ed.
        p. cm.
        1. English language—Textbooks for foreign speakers. 2. English
language—Spoken English—Problems, exercises, etc. 3. Listening—
Problems, exercises, etc. I. Title: Listening and Speaking, intermediate.
II. Schmidt, Jennifer. III. Title.

PE1128.S26 2003
428.3'4—dc21   2003044672

ISBN 0-201-75570-X (Student Book)
ISBN 0-13-143913-8 (Student Book with Audio CDs)

Printed in the United States of America
9 10—CRK—09 08 07 06
5 6 7 8 9 10—CRK—09 08 07 06

Contents

Welcome to NORTHSTAR

Second Edition

NorthStar leads the way in integrated skills series. The Second Edition remains an innovative, five-level series written for students with academic as well as personal language goals. Each unit of the thematically linked Reading and Writing strand and Listening and Speaking strand explores intellectually challenging, contemporary themes to stimulate critical thinking skills while building language competence.

Four easy to follow sections—Focus on the Topic, Focus on Reading/Focus on Listening, Focus on Vocabulary, and Focus on Writing/Focus on Speaking—invite students to focus on the process of learning through **NorthStar**.

Thematically Based Units

NorthStar engages students by organizing language study thematically. Themes provide stimulating topics for reading, writing, listening, and speaking.

Extensive Support to Build Skills for Academic Success

Creative activities help students develop language-learning strategies, such as predicting and identifying main ideas and details.

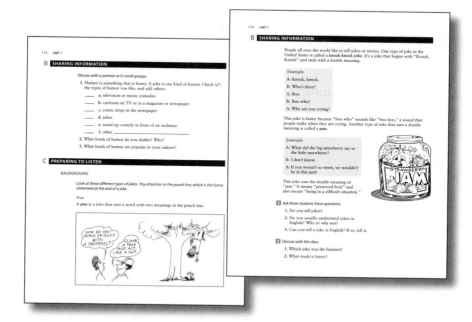

High-Interest Listening and Reading Selections

The two listening or reading selections in each unit present contrasting viewpoints to enrich students' understanding of the content while building language skills.

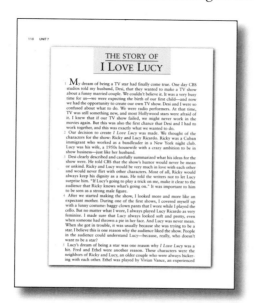

Critical Thinking Skill Development

Critical thinking skills, such as synthesizing information or reacting to the different viewpoints in the two reading or listening selections, are practiced throughout each unit, making language learning meaningful.

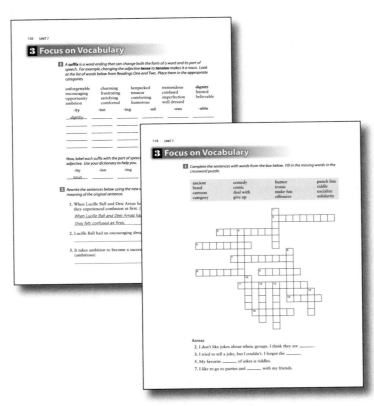

Extensive Vocabulary Practice

Students are introduced to key, contextualized vocabulary to help them comprehend the listening and reading selections. They also learn idioms, collocations, and word forms to help them explore, review, play with, and expand their spoken and written expression.

Powerful Pronunciation Practice

A carefully designed pronunciation syllabus in the Listening and Speaking strand focuses on topics such as stress, rhythm, and intonation. Theme-based pronunciation practice reinforces the vocabulary and content of the unit.

Content-Rich Grammar Practice

Each thematic unit integrates the study of grammar with related vocabulary and cultural information. The grammatical structures are drawn from the listening or reading selections and offer an opportunity for students to develop accuracy in speaking or writing about the topic.

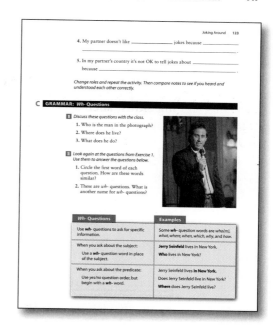

Extensive Opportunity for Discussion and Writing

Challenging and imaginative speaking activities, writing topics, and research assignments allow students to apply the language, grammar, style, and content they've learned.

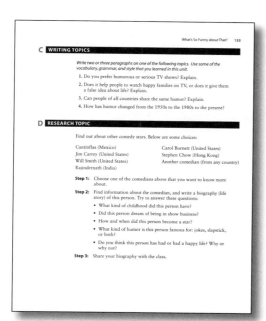

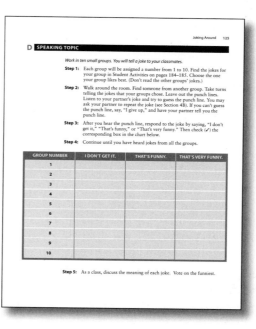

Writing Activity Book

The companion *Writing Activity Book* leads students through the writing process with engaging writing assignments. Skills and vocabulary from **NorthStar: Reading and Writing,** are reviewed and expanded as students learn the process of prewriting, organizing, revising, and editing.

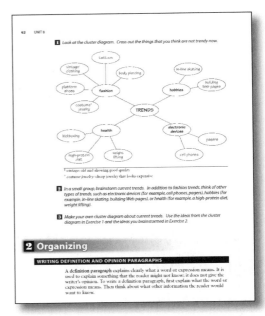

Audio Program

All the pronunciation, listening, and reading selections have been professionally recorded. The audio program includes audio CDs as well as audio cassettes.

Teacher's Manual with Achievement Tests

Each book in the series has an accompanying *Teacher's Manual* with step-by-step teaching suggestions, time guidelines, and expansion activities. Also included in each *Teacher's Manual* are reproducible unit-by-unit tests. The Listening and Speaking strand tests are recorded on CD and included in the *Teacher's Manual*. Packaged with each *Teacher's Manual* for the Reading and Writing strand is a TestGen CD-ROM that allows teachers to create and customize their own **NorthStar** tests. Answer Keys to both the Student Book and the Tests are included, along with a unit-by-unit word list of key vocabulary.

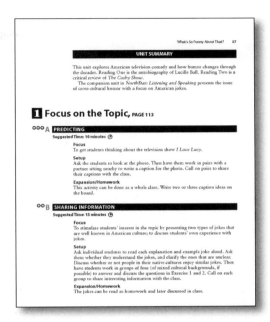

NorthStar Video Series

Engaging, authentic video clips, including cartoons, documentaries, interviews, and biographies correlate to the themes in **NorthStar.** There are four videos, one for each level of **NorthStar,** Second edition, containing 3- to 5- minute segments for each unit. Worksheets for the video can be found on the **NorthStar** Companion Website.

Companion Website

http://www.longman.com/northstar includes resources for students and teachers such as additional vocabulary activities, Web-based links and research, video worksheets, and correlations to state standards.

Scope and Sequence

Unit	Critical Thinking Skills	Listening Tasks
1 **Advertising on the Air** Theme: Advertising Listening One: *Advertising on the Air* A classroom lecture Listening Two: *Negative Appeals* Another excerpt from the lecture	Critique magazine and television ads Identify salient features of an ad Propose advertising campaigns according to market information Infer word meaning from context Support answers with information from the lecture Identify intended market of ads Compare and contrast advertising strategies Correlate examples with abstract principles	Identify chronology Listen for details Relate listenings to personal values Synthesize information from both listenings Identify emphasis in speech Listen to and evaluate student product promotions Identify message and strategy of student ads
2 **Pushing the Limit** Theme: Extreme Sports Listening One: *Journal of a Mountain Climber* An audio journal Listening Two: *Sensation Seekers* A psychology lecture	Challenge stereotypes Infer word meaning from context Support opinions with examples from the text Infer information not explicit in the text Correlate an individual example with broad trends Rank outdoor activities Analyze survey results	Identify main ideas Listen for details Interpret speaker's emotions Synthesize information from two listenings Distinguish between vowels sounds Listen for specific information in student responses Classify sounds Listen to student presentations and take notes
3 **Too Good to Be True** Theme: Fraud Listening One: *Too Good to Be True* A news report on fraud Listening Two: *Interviews* Four interviews with victims of fraud	Critique a solicitation from a con artist Theorize about the success of fraud Infer word meaning from context Support opinions with reasons Evaluate one's susceptibility to fraud Choose appropriate punishments for criminal acts Hypothesize outcomes	Identify chronology in a report Listen for details Interpret speaker's tone and emotions Support answers with information from the text Identify a con artist's strategies Listen for rhythm in speech Listen for reductions in speech View and critique a movie Listen to and comment on student research findings

Speaking Tasks	Pronunciation	Vocabulary	Grammar
Make predictions Propose advertising strategy Comment on ads using new vocabulary Read ads aloud with proper stress and intonation Promote a product with attention-grabbing language Offer advice using imperatives Create, rehearse, and perform a TV ad Record a two-minute summary of research	Highlighting words	Context clues Synonyms Definitions	Imperatives
Discuss interests in sports Construct and perform a dialogue using new vocabulary Elaborate extemporaneously on an idea Ask and answer questions about personal preferences Make travel suggestions Express and defend opinions Conduct a survey Present research on a sport	Front vowels /iy/, /ɪ/, /ey/, /ɛ/	Context clues Definitions Synonyms	Modals of preference
Describe types of fraud Share experiences Make predictions Recount experiences using new vocabulary Express and defend opinions Facilitate a group discussion Agree or disagree with statements Make comparative statements Present research findings on fraud	Reductions	Context clues Definitions	Equatives and comparatives

Unit	Critical Thinking Skills	Listening Tasks

4
The Art of Storytelling
Theme: Storytelling
Listening One: "Lavender"
   A story
Listening Two: *An Interview with Jackie Torrence*
   A conversation with a professional storyteller
	Interpret a photograph
	Express opinions about different types of storytelling
	Infer word meaning from context
	Analyze storytelling techniques
	Analyze and describe characters in a story
	Support opinions with reasons
	Match actions to their consequences
	Interpret meaning from text
		Listen for the main ideas
		Identify chronology in the story
		Interpret a speaker's emotions
		Synthesize information from two listenings
		Take a dictation
		Identify stress patterns in speech
		Listen for specific information in student responses
		Take notes on interviewee responses
		Listen to and evaluate student responses

5
Separated by the Same Language
Theme: Language
Listening One: *Accent and Identity*
   An interview
Listening Two: *Code Switching*
   A lecture on linguistics
	Interpret a cartoon
	Recognize personal bias and stereotypes about accents
	Classify information
	Infer word meaning from context
	Interpret word usage
	Hypothesize scenarios
	Infer information not explicit in the listenings
	Hypothesize another's point of view
	Analyze problems and propose solutions
		Listen for main ideas
		Listen for details
		Listen closely to interpret a speaker's emotions
		Relate listening to personal values
		Take notes on a lecture
		Integrate information from two listenings
		Listen for specific information in student responses

6
Culture and Commerce
Theme: Tourism
Listening One: *Radio News Report*
   A report on the Pa Daung tribe
Listening Two: *Town Hall Meeting in Hyannis, Cape Cod*
   Two opposing views on tourism
	Recognize personal assumptions about tourism
	Evaluate the advantages and disadvantages of tourism
	Infer word meaning from context
	Support opinions with reasons
	Hypothesize outcomes
	Compare and contrast vacation experiences
		Listen for main ideas
		Listen for details
		Interpret speaker's tone and emotions
		Identify contrasting viewpoints in the listening
		Synthesize information from two listenings
		Categorize end sounds
		Take a dictation
		Listen to student presentations and pose questions

7
Joking Around
Theme: Humor
Listening One: *What's So Funny?*
   An interview with a sociologist
Listening Two: *More Jokes*
   Eight jokes
	Interpret jokes
	Compare personal preferences in humor
	Infer word meaning from context
	Classify types of jokes
	Distinguish between ironic and non-ironic statements
	Draw conclusions
	Evaluate and rank quality of jokes
		Identify main ideas
		Listen for details
		Interpret speaker's tone of voice
		Compare observations in listening to one's personal observations
		Listen to jokes and predict punch lines
		Decipher words spoken with reduced pronunciation
		Take notes on student information

Speaking Tasks	Pronunciation	Vocabulary	Grammar
Make predictions Enhance storytelling with adjectives, adverbs, and details Practice composing descriptive sentences Make statements of purpose Collaborate to create, rehearse, and perform a story Record a summary of a story Conduct an interview	Rhythm of prepositional phrases	Context clues Word definitions Synonyms Dictionary work	Infinitives of purpose
Make predictions Pose and respond to questions Lead a group discussion Express and defend opinions Compare past and present abilities with modals Present a plan to improve English skills Present research on slang Conduct an interview and report findings	*Can/can't*	Word definitions Context clues	Modals of ability and possibility
Make predictions Express and defend opinions Use new vocabulary in an open conversation Tell a story using transition words Interview a classmate Summarize an interview Outline, rehearse, and present a three-minute speech Present a poster session about a local tourist attraction	Past tense endings	Context clues Word definitions Vocabulary classification	Simple past tense
Make predictions Give examples to illustrate new vocabulary Compose and tell original jokes Discuss preferences in entertainment Ask for repetition or clarification Ask and answer questions in an information gap activity Practice telling and reacting to jokes	Reduction of *h* in pronouns	Word definitions Phrasal verbs Context clues	*Wh-* questions

Unit	Critical Thinking Skills	Listening Tasks

8
 	
Traditional or Trendy?
Theme: Fashion
Listening One: *Interview with Shanika De Silva*
  A conversation about Sri Lankan fashion
Listening Two: *Interview with a Fashion Designer*
  A conversation about current fashion trends
	Compare and contrast two types of dress
	Compare cultural norms of dress
	Interpret word usage
	Analyze the advantages and disadvantages of traditional dress
	Hypothesize point of view
	Compare and contrast points of view
	Analyze relationships between words
	Interpret the significance of how a person dresses
		Identify main topics
		Listen for details
		Interpret speaker's attitude
		Relate listening to personal values
		Identify a speaker's point of view
		Synthesize information from two listenings
		Identify thought groups in speech
		Listen to student presentations and answer questions

9
 	
To Spank or Not to Spank?
Theme: Punishment
Listening One: *A Radio Report*
  A report on spanking
Listening Two: *Expert opinions*
  Three experts talk about spanking
	Recognize personal assumptions about spanking
	Infer word meaning from context
	Identify arguments for and against spanking
	Evaluate persuasiveness of arguments
	Analyze strategies speakers use to support their opinions
	Compare and contrast past and current childrearing practices
	Develop arguments in favor of or against an issue
		Determine a speaker's point of view
		Identify supporting ideas
		Take notes using a graphic organizer
		Listen for details
		Interpret a speaker's intensity of opinion
		Relate listening to personal values
		Synthesize information from two listenings
		Identify end sounds
		Listen for specific information in student responses

10
 	
Before You Say "I Do"
Theme: Marriage
Listening One: *A Prenuptial Agreement*
  An interview with newlyweds
Listening Two: *Reactions to the Prenuptial Agreement*
  Five opinions
	Interpret quotations
	Judge the value of a prenuptial agreement
	Infer word meaning from context
	Hypothesize another's point of view
	Support opinion with information from the text
	Develop arguments for and against an issue
	Evaluate the quality of arguments
		Identify main ideas
		Listen for details
		Determine a speaker's point of view
		Identify supporting reasons
		Listen for emphasis in speech
		Listen for student interruption strategies
		Listen closely to interpret meaning

Speaking Tasks	Pronunciation	Vocabulary	Grammar
Make predictions Express opinions Give impromptu definitions of new vocabulary Group words for appropriate intonation and meaning Manipulate intonation to change meaning of a sentence Describe changes in fashion using the phrase *used to* Outline, rehearse, and present an introduction to an oral report Give an impromptu presentation using an outline to quickly organize ideas and notes Give an oral report on research	Thought groups	Context clues Definitions Synonyms Analogies	*Used to*
Share background information Make predictions Make impromptu opinion statements using new vocabulary Support an opinion with facts, statistics, examples, and anecdotes Ask and answer questions Conduct a debate Express and defend opinions Use an outline to organize an argument Summarize observations on child discipline	Final consonants Tongue twisters	Word definitions Context clues Vocabulary classification	Present perfect tense
Make predictions Express and defend opinions Perform a role play using new vocabulary Use word stress to change the meaning of a sentence Practice interrupting politely Present a topic and lead a group discussion Conduct an oral history interview Research a topic and make a class presentation	Contrastive stress	Word definitions Context clues	Articles

Acknowledgments

We would like to express our gratitude to the many people who contributed to the materials and ideas for this book. In particular, we thank Serena Coorey, Meera Singh, and Camille Musser, whose interviews were the backbone of two of our units. Thanks also to San Khoo for travel information and pictures, and to the students at Portland State University for their feedback.

Special recognition goes to editors Frances Boyd, Carol Numrich, Deborah Lazarus, and Mykan White whose thoughtful perspectives and attention to detail helped to mold the manuscript into a text; and to Debbie Sistino who skillfully guided the project through its many incarnations. And finally, thanks to David Schmidt and Roy Solórzano for their support, encouragement, and hours of emergency babysitting throughout the writing process.

Helen S. Solórzano
Jennifer P. L. Schmidt

For her contribution in developing the NorthStar pronunciation syllabus, the publisher gratefully acknowledges the contribution of **Linda Lane**.

For the comments and insights they graciously offered to help shape the direction of the Second Edition of *NorthStar*, the publisher would like to thank all our **reviewers**. For a complete list of reviewers and institutions, see page 207.

Advertising on the Air

Is your printer really slow?

Work faster with Print Tech.
Printers for Home and Business.

1 Focus on the Topic

A PREDICTING

Discuss these questions with the class.

1. Look at the advertisement. What product is it selling?

2. Why does this ad use a photo of a turtle to sell the product? Do you think this ad would encourage people to buy the product? Why or why not?

3. Look at the title of the unit. What kind of advertising do you think this unit will be about?

B SHARING INFORMATION

Think of an ad that that you have seen or heard recently. Answer the questions. Share your answers in small groups.

1. Where did you see or hear the ad?

2. What product was the ad selling?

3. Why do you remember the ad? Choose one or more reasons to complete this sentence:

   I remember this ad because it had _____.

   - a funny situation

   - a good song

   - cartoons

   - nice-looking people

   - famous people

   - an unreal (fantasy) situation

   - a demonstration showing how the product works

   - (other) _____

C PREPARING TO LISTEN

BACKGROUND

1 *Read the information about radio advertising in the United States and look at the list of radio stations on page 3. What age group (teenagers, adults, older people) do you think listens to each radio station?*

Approximately 97% of Americans listen to the radio. Most people listen

   - every day

   - for three hours or more

   - to only two or three stations

   - while doing something else (exercising, working, etc.)

In 2000, advertisers spent $60 million on radio ads. Advertisers like radio because they can advertise to different markets.* For example, if a clothing company wants to advertise to teenagers, it can advertise on a radio station that plays pop music.

---

* **markets:** groups of people who may buy something

Radio Stations in the United States

99.2 WCLS Classical music
Classical music including Bach, Mozart, and Beethoven.

101.6 WBIZ Business news
Business news, stock market reports.

105 WHPP Pop music
Hip-hop and dance music.

106.9 WRCK Rock music
Rock music from the 1960s, 1970s, and 1980s.

2 *Choose one or two of the radio stations listed that are best for advertising each product. Explain why you chose those stations.*

PRODUCTS	RADIO STATIONS	WHY?
Cola		
Music CDs		
Computers		
Hair color		

VOCABULARY FOR COMPREHENSION

Match each underlined word with a definition or synonym listed below. Write the correct letter in the blank.

a. control

b. things that have power to make someone interested

c. ways to make us laugh

d. feelings

e. match

f. opinions about ourselves

g. make someone decide to do something

h. do one thing very well

i. high standard and expensive

j. special ways of doing things

_____ 1. Advertisers use our <u>emotions</u> to encourage us to buy products. They try to make us feel happy or sad, for example.

_____ 2. Advertisers try to <u>manipulate</u> our feelings so that we will buy their products.

_____ 3. Advertisers control our feelings by using emotional <u>appeals</u> that attract our attention.

_____ 4. We all like to hear funny stories, so advertisers often use <u>humor</u> in their ads.

_____ 5. It wouldn't be good to make a funny ad about a serious product. The ad wouldn't <u>fit</u> the product.

_____ 6. Some advertising companies <u>specialize</u>. For example, some companies create ads only for radio, while others create ads for TV.

_____ 7. I want him to buy a new car, but he says we don't need one. I'll show him this ad. That will <u>persuade</u> him.

_____ 8. Hilton hotels are <u>luxury</u> hotels. Their advertisements usually focus on furnishings, exercise facilities, restaurants, and service.

_____ 9. Sound effects, music, and songs are <u>techniques</u> that advertisers use to make their ads interesting and easy to remember.

_____ 10. Our <u>egos</u> make us want to look good in front of others.

2 Focus on Listening

A LISTENING ONE: *Advertising on the Air*

🎧 *Listen to the beginning of a lecture on advertising. Guess the best answer to complete each sentence. Discuss your answers with the class.*

1. This talk takes place _____.
   a. at a meeting
   b. in a college classroom
   c. on television

2. The rest of the listening will be about _____.
   a. the history of radio advertising
   b. radio versus TV advertising
   c. how advertisers manipulate emotions

LISTENING FOR MAIN IDEAS

🎧 **1** *Listen to the lecture. Put the emotional appeals in the order that you hear them. Mark them **1** (first) and **2** (second). One of the appeals is not mentioned. Then draw a line from the appeal to the product that the appeal is used to sell. One of the products is not mentioned.*

Emotional Appeals	Products Advertised
_____ humor	hair color
_____ romance	flea collar
_____ ego	fancy shampoo

2 *Circle the best answer to complete each sentence.*

1. The professor plays examples of radio ads _____ the lecture.
   a. at the beginning of   b. throughout   c. at the end of

2. The professor presents the information in _____ manner.
   a. an organized   b. a confusing   c. a formal

3. In this class there is _____ participation from the students.
   a. a lot of   b. some   c. no

LISTENING FOR DETAILS

Listen again. Circle the best answer to complete each sentence.

1. Last week the class talked about the _____ of radio advertising.
   a. effectiveness   **b.** history   **c.** cost

2. Advertisers manipulate our emotions by using _____.
   a. our attention   **b.** radio ads   **c.** emotional appeals

3. Humorous ads _____.
   a. are easy to remember   **b.** appeal to our egos   **c.** make us feel uncomfortable

4. Most flea treatments involve _____ with harsh chemicals.
   a. eating   **b.** bathing   **c.** combing

5. The Doggie's Friend flea collar has a _____ that fleas don't like.
   a. noise   **b.** smell   **c.** color

6. Advertisers don't make humorous ads for _____ products.
   a. expensive   **b.** funny   **c.** serious

7. People buy luxury cars so that they can look _____.
   a. strong   **b.** rich   **c.** safe

8. Kathy _____ a grandmother.
   a. is   **b.** is not   **c.** is hoping to be

9. It takes _____ minutes to get results from Younger You.
   a. 10   **b.** 7   **c.** 5

10. At the end of the listening, the professor says he will talk about _____.
    a. other appeals in advertising   **b.** other kinds of advertising   **c.** the cost of advertising

REACTING TO THE LISTENING

Before advertisers create ads, they have to decide what the market, or audience, will be. An ad may target, or focus on, men or women, young people or older people, and so on.

1 *Listen again to the advertisements in the lecture. On the chart, check (✓) the characteristics that describe the market for each ad. Write reasons for your choices. Give additional ideas for other markets in the section labeled "Other." Discuss your opinions with the class.*

MARKET(S) THAT THE AD TARGETS	DOGGIE'S FRIEND AD	REASONS	YOUNGER YOU AD	REASONS
Gender				
a. Male	❑		❑	
b. Female	❑		❑	
Age (in years)				
a. Birth–12	❑		❑	
b. 13–19	❑		❑	
c. 20–39	❑		❑	
d. 40–59	❑		❑	
e. 60 or older	❑		❑	
Income				
a. Below average	❑		❑	
b. Average	❑		❑	
c. Above average	❑		❑	
d. Rich	❑		❑	
Other				
_____	❑		❑	
_____	❑		❑	

2 *Discuss these questions with the class.*

1. The lecture discusses two emotional appeals used in advertising. In your opinion, is either one of these appeals more effective than the other? Why or why not?

2. Do you feel that it is all right for advertisers to use our emotions to get us to buy products? Why or why not?

3. How often do you listen to the radio? Are you influenced by (affected by) radio ads? Why or why not?

B LISTENING TWO: *Negative Appeals*

The appeals in Listening One focused on positive emotions. In Listening Two you will hear ads that use negative emotions.

🎧 *Listen to the two ads. Match each ad with an emotional appeal and write the letter in the blank. One of the appeals is not mentioned in the listening.*

Advertisement

_____ Thief Buster ad

_____ Rinse Away ad

Emotional Appeals

a. Embarrassment

b. Guilt

c. Fear

C LINKING LISTENINGS ONE AND TWO

Discuss the questions in pairs or small groups. Then share your ideas with the class.

1. Think of all the advertisements that you heard in Listening One and Listening Two. Which of the ads is the easiest for you to remember? Why is it memorable?

2. In Listening One, the professor talks about fitting the right emotional appeal to the right product.

   a. In the chart below, write the four products and the emotional appeals that were presented in Listenings One and Two. Then discuss why each appeal fits its product.

LISTENING ONE— DOGGIE'S FRIEND AD	LISTENING ONE— YOUNGER YOU AD	LISTENING TWO— THIEF BUSTER AD	LISTENING TWO— RINSE AWAY AD
Product:	Product:	Product:	Product:
Emotional appeal:	Emotional appeal:	Emotional appeal:	Emotional appeal:

b. If you produced advertisements, which appeals from Listenings One and Two would you use to sell each product below? Choose one or two appeals for each product and write them in the blanks. Share your choices with the class.

1. Diet pills   _____

2. Disinfectant spray
   (for killing germs in
   kitchens, bathrooms, etc.)   _____

3. Children's cookies   _____

4. Perfume   _____

3 Focus on Vocabulary

1 *A testimonial is a letter from a satisfied customer telling how great a product is. Read the following testimonial about Clayton's microwave dinners. Write the correct words in the blanks.*

Dear Clayton's,

My family loves your _____! Before we switched
                    1. (products / appeals)

to Clayton's I always felt _____ and
                          2. (humorous / guilty)

_____ about feeding my kids unhealthy food,
3. (embarrassed / manipulated)

but I didn't have time to cook. When I heard your

_____ on the radio and discovered that you
        4. (ad / ego)

_____ in healthy food, I decided to try your
    5. (target / specialize)

meals. They're great! The meals are delicious and they

_____ our busy lifestyle. Now I've got to think of
      6. (fit / manipulate)

some _____ to _____ my
         7. (techniques / emotions)   **8. (appeal / persuade)**

friends to try them!

                                        Traci Wennerholm

2 *Work in small groups. Look at the two advertisements below and discuss these questions for each ad. Remember to use the underlined words during your discussion.*

1. What <u>product</u> does this company <u>specialize</u> in?

2. Who is the <u>target market</u> for this <u>ad</u>?

3. What type of <u>emotional appeal(s)</u> does this ad use? (You may suggest appeals not presented in this unit.)

4. Does the emotional appeal <u>fit</u> the product? Why or why not?

5. Do you think this ad is <u>effective</u>? Why or why not?

Advertisement 1

Advertisement 2

4 Focus on Speaking

A   PRONUNCIATION: Highlighting

In radio ads, the actors emphasize, or highlight, certain words to help us focus on important information. The same pattern occurs in all kinds of communication. When we speak, we emphasize certain words to make our meaning clear.

🎧 *Listen to the following excerpt from Listening One. Notice how the speakers highlight important information.*

LIZ: It's **AMAZING!** You really **DO** look younger!

KATHY: **THANKS! NOW** people don't believe I'm a **GRANDMOTHER.**

LIZ: I should try it.

To highlight or emphasize a word in a sentence, use strong stress.

- Say the word with a higher pitch (tone).
- Say the word louder.
- Say the word longer.

1 *Read the following conversations. Circle the words that you think will be highlighted.*

1. KATHY: Hello?

   LIZ: Kathy! I took your advice.

   KATHY: What advice?

   LIZ: I colored my hair.

   KATHY: With Younger You?

   LIZ: Yes! It's great!

2. KATHY: Did you hear about that new flea collar?

   LIZ: Yes, I'm going to the pet store today. How about you?

   KATHY: I think I'll stop by tomorrow.

🎧 *Listen to the conversations and check your answers. Compare your answers with a partner's.*

2 *Work with a partner on the following activity.*

Student A

1. Look at Ad 1 below. You are going to read the ad to your partner two times. Circle the important information that you will highlight. Highlight the words you have circled by saying them louder, longer, and/or with a high pitch and strong stress.

2. Listen as Student B reads Ad 2 below. Circle the words that your partner highlights.

Student B

1. Listen as Student A reads Ad 1. Circle the words that your partner highlights.

2. Look at Ad 2. Circle the words you will highlight. Read the ad to your partner two times. Highlight the words you have circled by saying them louder, longer, and/or with a high pitch and strong stress.

When you are finished, compare your answers. Did you circle the same words? Discuss any differences.

Advertisement 1

Advertisement 2

Now find another partner and repeat the exercise. This time switch ads. (Student A reads Ad 2. Student B reads Ad 1.)

B STYLE: Attention Grabbers

Attention grabbers are techniques that you can use to "grab" a listener's attention or make a person want to listen to you. These techniques are often used in advertising. When you give an oral presentation, you can use one of the following attention grabbers at the beginning of your presentation.

Attention Grabbers	Examples
a. Give the solution to a problem.	"Dinnertime can be busy and stressful for all of us, especially if it's late and the kids are hungry. . . . Well, *now* there's a solution . . ."
b. Ask a question.	"Do you find dinnertime stressful?"
c. Tell an anecdote (short story).	"Dinnertime was always stressful at my house. I'd run in late from work and search desperately through the fridge for something quick to cook, while the kids demanded my attention . . ."
d. Give a dramatic fact or statistic.	"In the United States, 70 percent of families say that dinnertime is stressful."

Note: Techniques can be combined. For example, a question can be followed by an anecdote.

1 *Read the following attention grabbers for a presentation on advertising. Write the letter of the technique from the chart above.*

_____ 1. "In 1998, advertisers in the United States spent $15.4 billion on radio advertising."

_____ 2. "As I was listening to my favorite radio program the other day, an ad caught my attention. It was a song about a special kind of coffee, and before I knew what was happening, I started singing along."

_____ 3. "If you're like I am, you probably enjoy listening to the radio but hate the ads. Well, if you start to think of the ads as entertainment, you might start to enjoy them."

_____ 4. "Have you ever wondered how advertisers get ideas for their ads?"

Compare your answers with a partner's and discuss any differences.

2 *Work with a partner. Write a few lines of an advertisement for a product from the list below. Write more than one ad, each with a different attention grabber.*

Products

Hawaiian vacation package
toothpaste
laundry detergent
ear plugs

With the class, discuss the attention grabbers for each product. When your product is discussed, read the attention grabber for your advertisement.

After everyone has read their attention grabbers, discuss these questions:

- Which is the most interesting attention grabber for each product?

- What makes it the most interesting?

C   GRAMMAR: Imperatives

Imperatives are often used to give orders or suggestions. Advertisers use imperatives to get people's attention and to make their message simple and direct.

1 *Read the following excerpt from the Doggie's Friend advertisement. Underline the imperative forms.*

"Don't delay. Get a Doggie's Friend today."

Imperatives	Examples
To form an imperative: • Omit the subject. • Use the base form of the verb.	"**Get** a Doggie's Friend today."
To form a negative imperative: • Put *don't* before the base form of the verb.	"**Don't delay.**"

2 *Divide into two groups, A and B. Each group stands in a line so that Group A faces Group B.*

Group A

1. Choose a problem from the list. Tell the student in Group B (standing opposite you) your problem and ask for advice. The Group B student will make a suggestion.

   Problems

   My dog has fleas.
   My hair is turning gray.
   My dining table has a broken leg.
   I get home late every day and never have time to make dinner.
   I'm tired of work. I need a vacation.
   I have a new car, and I'm afraid someone is going to steal it.

   Example: GROUP A STUDENT: My dog has fleas. What can I do?

   GROUP B STUDENT: Try a flea collar. Don't use chemicals!

2. After Student B has made a suggestion, move along the line and ask the next student in Group B the same question. Keep moving down the line until you have spoken to all the students from Group B.

3. Decide what advice you like best. Be prepared to report to the class if your teacher calls on you.

Group B

Listen to the problems Group A students choose. Make suggestions using imperatives.

   Example: GROUP A STUDENT: My dog has fleas. What can I do?

   GROUP B STUDENT: Try a flea collar. Don't use chemicals!

Now switch roles so that Group B asks and Group A answers.

D SPEAKING TOPIC

Work in small groups to create your own TV advertisement. You will perform your ad for the class.

PREPARING

Complete the worksheet on page 16 with your group. Each group member should have his or her own copy.

WORKSHEET FOR TV AD

1. **What product would you like to sell?**

2. **What will the product be used for?**

3. **What is the name of the product?**

4. **Which emotional appeal will you use?**
   (Suggestions: humor, ego, fear, guilt, embarrassment)

5. **Which attention grabber will you use (see Section 4B)?**

Now write the ad, using your completed worksheet as a guide.

- Make sure that every group member has a speaking part. Be creative!
- Keep your ad short. Try to fit it on one sheet of paper.
- Use imperatives to make your message simple and direct (see Section 4C).
- Make a script with all the speaking parts. Each group member should have his or her own copy.

PRACTICING

Practice for the performance.

- Read through the script and underline important words to emphasize.
- Rehearse the performance. Remember to use correct word stress (see Section 4A).
- Try to memorize your part so that you don't need to look at your script.

PERFORMING

Perform your advertisement for the class. You may use costumes and props to make your presentations more entertaining. The performances can be videotaped or audiotaped.

Listening Task

As you listen to the presentations, find the answers to the following questions.

1. What product is this ad selling?

2. What attention grabber is this ad using?

3. What emotional appeal is this ad using?

E   RESEARCH TOPICS

LOOKING AT MAGAZINE ADS

Step 1: Find three magazine ads that illustrate some of the emotional appeals discussed in the unit (humor, ego, fear, embarrassment). Bring the ads to class.

Step 2: Show your ads to a small group of students. As a group, discuss the following questions.

1. What emotional appeal(s) is the advertiser using?

2. Why is the advertiser using this appeal to sell this product?

3. Who is the target market?

4. Do you think this ad is effective? Why or why not?

Step 3: Show your ads to the class and present the results of your discussion.

LOOKING AT TV ADS

Step 1: Watch three different kinds of TV shows—for example, the news, a cartoon, and a soap opera. Make a list of the products that appear in the ads during these shows. Videotape the ads if possible. Take brief notes to answer the following questions.

1. Were different products advertised on different shows? Give examples.

2. Why do advertisers choose certain shows for their ads?

3. What was your favorite ad? Tell what happened in the ad. Say why you liked it.

Step 2:   Before class, make a tape recording of your observations. Speak for about two minutes. (Don't write out your comments ahead of time; just speak clearly and naturally.) Give the tape to your teacher for feedback.

Step 3:   In class, meet in groups of four. Make a list of the kinds of TV shows that every group member watched. Choose one type of show that all or most of the group watched. Discuss the questions that you answered in your research.

Step 4:   Share your answers with the class.

For Unit 1 Internet activities, visit the NorthStar Companion Website at http://www.longman.com/northstar.

Pushing the Limit

1 Focus on the Topic

A PREDICTING

Discuss these questions with the class.

1. Look at the photo. What is this person doing? Is it dangerous? Why or why not?

2. What do you think the title of this unit means? What do you think this unit will be about?

B SHARING INFORMATION

Discuss these questions in small groups. Then share your answers with the class.

1. Do you enjoy "pushing the limit" and doing something that is dangerous (for example, rock climbing, parachuting, bungee jumping)? Why or why not?

2. What activities have you done that have "pushed the limit"?

C PREPARING TO LISTEN

BACKGROUND

Read the information about the dangers of climbing Mount Shasta.

Climbing Mount Shasta: Risks and Safety Suggestions

At 14,162 feet (4,317 meters), Mount Shasta is one of the largest mountains in Northern California. Although it takes only two days to hike to the top, the climb involves some danger. Every year there are accidents that result in injury or death on this mountain.

Avalanches: At any time of the year, large amounts of snow and ice can come down the mountain on top of climbers. Don't climb in the winter, when the risk is the highest.

Rock falls: Every day, rocks break off and roll down the mountain. When climbing, look up ahead for falling rocks. Stay away from areas where the rocks look like they could come loose.

Weather: The weather on Shasta can change very quickly. Check the weather before you begin your climb. If a storm comes in while you are climbing, go down the mountain immediately.

Mountain sickness: Many people get headaches and feel weak when climbing high mountains. To avoid mountain sickness, drink plenty of water and don't hike too fast. If you get a strong headache or dizziness, and have great trouble breathing or walking, go down the mountain immediately.

Hypothermia and Frostbite: Hypothermia can happen if your body gets too cold and cannot heat itself up. Frostbite occurs when your fingers, toes, and face get so cold they freeze. Make sure that you have the correct clothing for snow climbing.

Discuss the following questions.

1. In your opinion, how dangerous is it to climb Mount Shasta?
   a. not dangerous   c. dangerous
   b. somewhat dangerous   d. very dangerous

2. What kind of person do you think would like to climb this mountain?

3. Would you climb Mount Shasta? Why or why not?

VOCABULARY FOR COMPREHENSION

Circle the best answer to complete the definition of each underlined word.

1. In the morning, the climber began her <u>ascent</u> of the mountain. She reached the top by the afternoon.

   An <u>ascent</u> is a _____.
   a. climb up   b. fall down   c. turn around

2. The top of the mountain looked close, but it was <u>deceiving</u>. Actually, it was very far away.

   When something is <u>deceiving</u>, it _____.
   a. is true   b. cannot be trusted   c. is clear

3. My <u>goal</u> is to climb Mount Everest, the highest mountain in the world. I hope to climb it next year.

   A <u>goal</u> is something that you _____.
   a. have already done   b. are doing right now   c. want to do

4. She <u>planted</u> her foot in the snow before taking a step.

   To <u>plant</u> a foot means to _____.
   a. put the foot down   b. lift the foot up   c. touch the foot to
      strongly   carefully   something

5. She listened to the radio so that she could walk with the <u>rhythm</u> of the music.

   A <u>rhythm</u> is a _____.
   a. way of walking   b. pattern of sound   c. type of music

6. She was so cold that she felt no <u>sensation</u> in her hands or feet. She didn't feel anything.

   A <u>sensation</u> means _____.
   a. warmth   b. tiredness   c. feeling

Circle the picture that best shows the meaning of the underlined words.

7. The climber brought an <u>axe</u> to cut into the snow and ice.

   a.   b.   c.

8. It is difficult to walk up the mountain because it is very <u>steep</u>.

   a.   b.   c.

9. She walked <u>diagonally</u> up the hill, from the left at the bottom to the top at the right.

a.   b.   c.

10. After climbing all day, she reached the <u>ridge</u> near the top of the mountain.

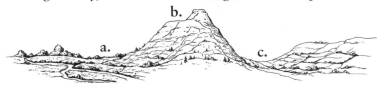

2 Focus on Listening

A LISTENING ONE: *Journal of a Mountain Climber*

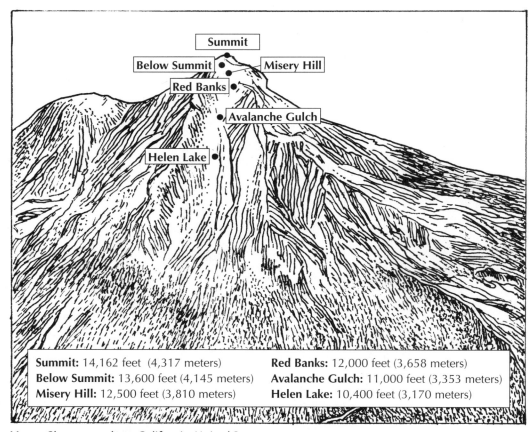

Summit: 14,162 feet (4,317 meters)	**Red Banks:** 12,000 feet (3,658 meters)
Below Summit: 13,600 feet (4,145 meters)	**Avalanche Gulch:** 11,000 feet (3,353 meters)
Misery Hill: 12,500 feet (3,810 meters)	**Helen Lake:** 10,400 feet (3,170 meters)

Mount Shasta, northern California, United States

Listen to an excerpt from Listening One. You will hear an audio journal made by Jennifer Ulman while she climbed Mount Shasta. Where do you think Jennifer is on the mountain during this excerpt? Why?

1. at the bottom

2. in the middle

3. at the top

LISTENING FOR MAIN IDEAS

Listen to the audio journal. Mark the statements T (true) or F (false).

Jennifer . . .

_____ 1. climbed part of the mountain the day before this recording.

_____ 2. is climbing alone.

_____ 3. is climbing in the morning.

_____ 4. hurt her foot during the climb.

_____ 5. is climbing on snow and ice.

_____ 6. does not reach the summit of the mountain.

LISTENING FOR DETAILS

Listen again. Circle the best answer to complete each sentence.

1. Helen Lake: Jennifer's body hurts from _____.
   a. climbing today   b. yesterday's climb   c. sitting down too long

2. Avalanche Gulch: When climbing, Jennifer plants her ice axe _____.
   a. in front of her   b. to the side   c. in back of her

3. Avalanche Gulch: Jennifer uses a _____ to help her climb.
   a. song   b. rhythm   c. story

4. Red Banks: Jennifer _____ the mountain.
   a. slips and almost falls down   b. turns around and walks down   c. sits down and rests on

5. Misery Hill: The weather on Misery Hill is _____.
   a. rainy   b. windy   c. deceiving

6. Misery Hill: Jennifer thinks about _____.
   a. eating lunch   b. her tired legs   c. life at home

7. Below the summit: Jennifer feels _____.

  a. a rush of energy   **b.** almost too tired   **c.** like turning around and
                                  to climb   going home

8. Below the summit: There are _____ members of the group ahead of
  Jennifer.

  a. no   **b.** two   **c.** three

9. At the summit: Tom _____ Jennifer and Doug.

  a. sings to   **b.** laughs with   **c.** takes a photo of

10. At the summit: Jennifer sees _____ below her.

  a. the other climbers   **b.** an airplane flying **c.** a snowstorm

REACTING TO THE LISTENING

 1 *Listen to the excerpts. Write down the key words that Jennifer uses to show how she is feeling. Then circle the words that describe her manner of speaking. Finally, circle the adjective you think best describes her feelings in each excerpt. Be prepared to explain the reasons for your choices.*

	HOW JENNIFER SHOWS HER FEELINGS		JENNIFER'S FEELINGS
	KEY WORDS	**MANNER OF SPEAKING**	
Excerpt 1		**Volume** **Speed** loud fast medium medium soft slow	frightened strong tired excited
Excerpt 2		**Volume** **Speed** loud fast medium medium soft slow	frightened strong tired excited
Excerpt 3		**Volume** **Speed** loud soft medium medium soft slow	frightened strong tired excited

2 *Discuss these questions with the class.*

1. Do you think Jennifer enjoyed her climb up Mount Shasta? Use examples from the listening to support your opinion. Do you think she would do it again?

2. Would you enjoy the same climb? Why or why not?

B   LISTENING TWO: *Sensation Seekers*

A "seeker" is someone who looks for something. Listen to a psychology lecture about people who are "sensation seekers." Choose the best answer to complete the statements.

1. Sensation seekers like _____ emotions.
   a. strong
   b. happy
   c. unhealthy

2. For example, according to the listening they like rock music, _____, and extreme sports.
   a. fast cars
   b. horror movies
   c. spicy food

3. Sensation seekers also like _____ experiences.
   a. difficult
   b. new
   c. repeated

4. For example, they like _____ and extreme sports.
   a. unpredictable jobs
   b. traveling
   c. fast cars

C   LINKING LISTENINGS ONE AND TWO

1 *Is the climber in Listening One a "sensation seeker"? Why or why not? Find examples from the listening to support your opinion. Discuss your thoughts in groups. Then share your answers with the class.*

2 *Work in small groups. Use the information from Listenings One and Two to create a description of Jennifer Ulman in the chart on page 26. Be sure to explain your ideas. Share your description with the class.*

	DESCRIPTION	EXPLANATION
Age		
Job		
Level of education		
Income		
Marital status		

3 Focus on Vocabulary

1 *Work with a partner. Read the journal entries from one of Jennifer's mountain-climbing trips. Complete the sentences with words from the boxes below. There is one extra word in each box.*

ascent	climb	experience	summit
axe	diagonally	steep	

August 12   We started our **(1)**_____ today. We
hope to reach the **(2)**_____ in two days, if all goes
well. We plan to go **(3)**_____ across the mountain
instead of straight up because it is an easier climb.
        After lunch, we had to **(4)**_____ some icy
rocks. It was very **(5)**_____—almost straight up.
By the time I got to the top, I was <u>so</u> tired. So far, this trip has
been a great **(6)**_____. I'm pushing my limits, but
it's really fun!!

deceiving	goal	rhythm	sensation
frightening	plant	ridge	

August 13   This mountain is **(7)**_____. Just

when you think you are at the top, there is another

(8)_____ in front of you. But you have to keep

going—just **(9)**_____ one foot in front of another .

. . keep the 1-2-3 **(10)**_____ of climbing.

   We reached our **(11)**_____ around noon—the

summit. What a great feeling!! Standing there, I had the

(12)_____ of being at the top of the world. I could

see for miles.

2 *Work in pairs. One person is a mountain climber from Jennifer Ulman's climb up Mount Shasta. The other person is a friend who did not climb the mountain. Write a dialogue together. The friend asks questions about climbing Mount Shasta. The mountain climber answers the questions.*

- Try to make your dialogue about two minutes long.

- Use the information from Listening One or add your own ideas about what the mountain-climbing trip was like.

- Use the words from the list below. Try to use each word at least once.

Nouns		Verbs	Adjectives	
ascent	rhythm	climb	dangerous	frightening
axe	ridge	plant	exciting	steep
experience	sensation	push the limits	extreme	
goal	summit			

Example: FRIEND: How did you like **climbing** Mount Shasta?

                 MOUNTAIN CLIMBER: It was very **exciting**! But I really had to **push my limits.**

Practice the dialogue. Then perform it for the class.

4 Focus on Speaking

A   PRONUNCIATION: Front Vowels /iy/, /ɪ/, /ey/, /ɛ/

*Listen to the words **read, rich, pain,** and **pen** as you look at the pictures of the vowel sounds in these words. The difference between the vowels in* reach *and* rich *is similar to the difference between the vowels in* pain *and* pen.

reach /iy/

• Your lips are spread.

• This vowel ends in a /y/ sound.

rich /ɪ/

• Your lips are not spread.

• Inside your mouth, your tongue is lower for /ɪ/ than for /iy/.

pain /ey/

• Your lips are spread.

• This vowel ends in a /y/ sound.

pen /ɛ/

• Your lips are not spread.

• Inside your mouth, your tongue is lower for /ɛ/ than for /ey/.

 1 *Listen to the words and repeat them.*

1. reach	rich	**6.** main	men
2. pain	pen	**7.** fail	fell
3. miss	mess	**8.** pit	pet
4. sit	set	**9.** seat	sit
5. reason	risen	**10.** seek	sick

 2 *Listen again. You will hear one word from each pair in Exercise 1. Circle the word you hear.*

3 *Work with a partner. Student A says a word from one of the pairs in Exercise 1. Student B points to the word and repeats it. Continue with the rest of the pairs. Switch roles and repeat the activity.*

 4 *Listen to the phrases and repeat. The underlined vowels are /iy/, /ɪ/, /ey/, and /ɛ/. Write each phrase under the matching vowel pattern in the chart.*

1. a d<u>ee</u>p br<u>ea</u>th
2. k<u>ee</u>p the rh<u>y</u>thm
3. r<u>i</u>sk t<u>a</u>kers
4. w<u>i</u>ndy w<u>ea</u>ther
5. a st<u>ee</u>p asc<u>e</u>nt

6. a l<u>i</u>ttle r<u>e</u>st
7. sens<u>a</u>tion s<u>ee</u>kers
8. a st<u>ee</u>p h<u>i</u>ll
9. the thr<u>i</u>ll of d<u>a</u>nger
10. my f<u>a</u>vorite p<u>eo</u>ple

reach	**pen**		**pain**	**reach**
/iy/	/ɛ/		/ey/	/iy/
a deep breath			_____	
_____			_____	

rich	**pen**		**rich**	**pain**
/ɪ/	/ɛ/		/ɪ/	/ey/
_____			_____	
_____			_____	

reach	**rich**
/iy/	/ɪ/
_____	
_____	

Check your answers with a partner's and take turns saying the phrases.

B | **STYLE: Giving Reasons and Elaborating**

To explain your ideas and opinions, you can give reasons.

Examples

- Mountain climbing is my favorite sport **because I** enjoy the changes in scenery.

- **One reason** mountain climbing is my favorite sport **is because** it's very strenuous.

- I like mountain climbing **because I** get out into the fresh air.

It is often helpful to *elaborate* on your reasons. You can do this by explaining in more detail, such as giving examples or more description.

Example

> Mountain climbing is my favorite sport **because** I enjoy the changes in scenery as I go up. When I begin a climb I'm usually in the trees. As I go higher there are bushes, and eventually, there's just rock and snow. It's really interesting.

Sit in a circle with a small group. Read question 1. Go around the circle so that each student gives an answer. Remember to (1) give your idea or opinion, (2) say your reason(s), and (3) elaborate. Continue in the same way with the other questions.

1. What is your favorite sport to watch? Why?

2. What kind of exercise do you enjoy doing? Why?

3. Do you enjoying doing an extreme sport? If so, what sport is it, and why do you like it? If not, why don't you like extreme sports?

4. What is the most popular extreme sport in your country? Why?

5. What is the most popular team sport in your country? Why?

6. Is there a sport that is impossible to do in your country? If so, what is it and why is it impossible to do?

Share your small-group discussions with the class.

C   GRAMMAR: Modals of Preference

1 *Read the dialogue between two mountain climbers. Underline the phrases that ask about or express a preference.*

DAVE: <u>Would you prefer</u> to keep climbing, or would you rather rest?

JENNIFER: Let's keep climbing. I'd rather not stop right now.

DAVE: I'll make dinner when we get to Lake Helen. Would you prefer beef stew or rice and beans?

JENNIFER: Usually, I prefer rice and beans to beef stew. But today I'm really hungry. I'd rather have beef stew.

Modals of Preference	Examples
Use **prefer**, **would prefer**, and **would rather** to talk about activities that you like better than other activities.	**I'd rather** go hiking than go mountain climbing. (*Would* is often shortened in statements.)
Prefer and **would prefer** may be followed by a noun, a gerund, or an infinitive.	I prefer **football**. I prefer **playing** football. I'd prefer **to play** football.
A comparison with **to** may also follow **prefer / would prefer** + noun or **prefer / would prefer** + gerund.	I prefer hiking **to** mountain climbing. I'd prefer going hiking **to** climbing a mountain.
Would rather can be followed only by the base form of the verb.	I'd rather **swim**.
A comparison with **than** may also follow **would rather**.	I'd rather swim **than** ski.
Use **rather not** to refuse an offer, suggestion, or invitation.	A: Would you like to go skiing? B: **I'd rather not.** I think I'm getting a cold.

2 *Work in pairs. Plan an adventure trip for your partner. Use the modals of preference listed below and on page 32 to find out what arrangements and activities your partner prefers. Student A asks Student B which things he or she prefers, and why. Student A checks off Student B's answers on the list. Then switch roles and repeat.*

Example: STUDENT A: Do you **prefer** to travel alone or with a group?

STUDENT B: I prefer to travel in a group.

STUDENT A: Why do you **prefer** a group?

STUDENT B: Because I get lonely when I'm by myself.

1. **prefer**
   ❑ travel alone   ❑ travel with a group

2. **would rather**
   ❑ go in the summer   ❑ go in the winter

3. **would prefer**

❑ a short trip   ❑ a long trip

4. **prefer**

❑ push yourself   ❑ take it slow

5. **would prefer**

❑ go with a guide   ❑ guide yourself

6. **would rather**

❑ do something dangerous   ❑ do something safe

7. **would rather**

❑ use equipment   ❑ not use equipment

8. **prefer**

❑ _____   ❑ _____

Based on the information you gathered, list three possible adventure trips for your partner. Share them with your partner. Does your partner like your suggestions?

Possible adventure trips: _____

_____

_____

D   SPEAKING TOPIC

Work in small groups to give your opinions about different extreme sports.

Step 1:   Discuss the following activities and how you feel about them. Which activities would you prefer to do? Which would you rather not do? (Use language from Section 4C.) Give reasons for your opinions. (Use language from Section 4B.) Take notes on the discussion.

Activities

mountain climbing

parachuting

hot-air ballooning

bungee jumping

skiing

Which activity is the most . . . ?

- dangerous
- exciting
- difficult
- relaxing
- uncomfortable
- expensive

Step 2: Compare the opinions of your group with those of the class.

1. Do the groups agree about each activity? Why or why not?

2. How many people in the class would like to try each activity? How many would not? Why?

3. Based on the opinions of everyone in the class, discuss which people are "sensation seekers" and which people are not "sensation seekers"? How can you tell?

E   RESEARCH TOPICS

EXTREME SPORTS SURVEY

Step 1: Interview three people from outside your class about their experience with difficult and dangerous sports. Write down each interviewee's name, age, and gender in the survey on page 34. Then use the questions listed below to ask them about each of the sports listed in the survey. Add one sport of your own to the list. Record your answers in the survey.

Questions

1. Have you ever gone _____ (name of sport)?

2. If yes, would you like to try it again?

   Why or why not? What did you like/dislike about _____ (name of sport)?

3. If no, would you like to try it? Why or why not? What makes you

   want/not want to try _____ (name of sport)?

Step 2: In small groups, analyze the results of your survey. Compare the answers of the students in the group.

1. Did men and women answer the questions differently? How?

2. Did people of different ages answer the questions differently? How?

3. Which sport have the most people tried?

4. Which sport have the least people tried?

5. Did you find anything surprising about the answers?

SURVEY

Interviewee 1: _____ Age: _____ Gender: _____

Interviewee 2: _____ Age: _____ Gender: _____

Interviewee 3: _____ Age: _____ Gender: _____

Have you ever gone . . .

	Mountain Climbing		White-Water Rafting		Skate-boarding		Hot-Air Ballooning		Bungee Jumping		(Other) _____	
	Yes	No	Yes	No	Yes	No	Yes	No	Yes	No	Yes	No
Interviewee 1	❑	❑	❑	❑	❑	❑	❑	❑	❑	❑	❑	❑
Interviewee 2	❑	❑	❑	❑	❑	❑	❑	❑	❑	❑	❑	❑
Interviewee 3	❑	❑	❑	❑	❑	❑	❑	❑	❑	❑	❑	❑

Want to try (again)?

Interviewee 1	❑	❑	❑	❑	❑	❑	❑	❑	❑	❑	❑	❑
Interviewee 2	❑	❑	❑	❑	❑	❑	❑	❑	❑	❑	❑	❑
Interviewee 3	❑	❑	❑	❑	❑	❑	❑	❑	❑	❑	❑	❑

Do not want to try

Interviewee 1	❑	❑	❑	❑	❑	❑	❑	❑	❑	❑	❑	❑
Interviewee 2	❑	❑	❑	❑	❑	❑	❑	❑	❑	❑	❑	❑
Interviewee 3	❑	❑	❑	❑	❑	❑	❑	❑	❑	❑	❑	❑

Reason

Interviewee 1					
Interviewee 2					
Interviewee 3					

RESEARCH ON EXTREME SPORTS

Step 1:   Choose a sport to research. You can select a sport from the following list or think of your own. Each student should research a different sport.

Sports

base jumping
bungee jumping
go-cart racing
hang gliding
hot-air ballooning
indoor rock climbing
inline skating
jet skiing
mountain biking

paintball
parachuting
parasailing
river kayaking
river rafting
ropes course
skateboarding
——————— (your choice)

Step 2:   Find out about the sport that you chose. Do research in the library or on the Internet, or talk to a local athlete who does the sport. Find out:

- How to do the sport

- The dangers of the sport

- Why people like the sport

- Where or if you can do the sport locally

Step 3:   Give a short presentation to the class about the sport.

Listening Task

Take notes as you listen to the other presentations. Be prepared to explain which sport you would most like to do and which sport you would not like to do, and why.

For Unit 2 Internet activities, visit the NorthStar Companion Website at
http://www.longman.com/northstar.

Too Good to Be True

Dear Tony,

Congratulations!

You are the lucky winner of
the Great Vacation Sweepstakes!*
You have already won
a fabulous vacation to

BALI!

To receive your prize . . .

1 Focus on the Topic

A PREDICTING

Read the letter. Discuss these questions with the class.

1. What do you think you have to do to get the trip to Bali? Do you think this letter is honest? Why or why not?

2. What does the title of this unit mean?

---

*sweepstakes: a competition in which you have a chance to win a prize if your name is chosen

B   SHARING INFORMATION

The letter you read in Section 1A is an example of **fraud**. Fraud is a type of crime in which the criminal lies to someone in order to get money.

1 *Work in small groups. Look at the list of different types of fraud, or scams. Discuss each kind of fraud and write a description of it on the blanks. Then think of two more scams to add to the list.*

1. **Identity theft**

   when someone uses your personal information (name, address, etc.) to get

   credit cards or cash checks

2. **Sweepstakes scam**

   _____

   _____

3. **Medical fraud**

   _____

   _____

4. **Internet fraud**

   _____

   _____

5. _____

   _____

   _____

6. _____

   _____

   _____

2 *Have you ever been a victim of fraud or do you know someone who has? Put a check (✓) next to the kinds of fraud in Exercise 1 that you have experienced or heard about.*

C   PREPARING TO LISTEN

BACKGROUND

Read the following paragraphs and look at the statistics about telemarketing fraud. Then discuss the questions with the class.

Telemarketing fraud is one of the most common types of fraud. In telemarketing fraud, a dishonest "telemarketer" telephones people and tricks them into sending money. People send money because they believe that they will get something in return. All the telemarketer needs is a telephone and a list of phone numbers. Working on the phone for eight hours a day, a criminal telemarketer can steal thousands of dollars.

Once people become victims of telemarketing fraud, they are asked to send money for more and more scams. When dishonest telemarketers find victims who will send them money, they sell their names to other dishonest telemarketers. Soon, the victims are receiving several phone calls each day. Some people can easily lose all their money before the calls stop.

FRAUD FACTS

Telemarketing Fraud in the United States

$1,425	Amount the average victim loses per year
50%	Percentage of fraud victims age 50 and older
14,000	Number of illegal telemarketing companies

Top Three Telemarketing Frauds

#1 Sweepstakes

#2 Magazine subscription sales

#3 New credit card offers

Discussion Questions

1. Why do you think so many people over age 50 are victims of fraud?

2. Why do you think telemarketing fraud is so common?

VOCABULARY FOR COMPREHENSION

Read the following letter and paragraphs. Match each underlined word with one of the definitions that follow. Write the number in the blank. Compare your answers with a partner's.

Dear Tony,

Congratulations! You have just won a luxury vacation to BALI! Your trip includes seven nights at the most expensive hotel and meals at the finest restaurants. You'll live like a king for a week!

To get your (**1**) <u>prize</u>—a free BALI vacation—please send a $500 (**2**) <u>deposit</u> right away to the address below.

When we receive the deposit, we will send you more information about your vacation! (Your money will be returned if you decide not to go.)

Sincerely,

SUNSHINE VACATIONS
703 Western Avenue
Miami, Florida 33102

You've just received this letter in the mail. Ask yourself, Do you (**3**) <u>trust</u> this letter? Do you think it's true? Many people would say yes, and they would lose their money. They may become (**4**) <u>victims</u> of a crime called fraud. Most people are very embarrassed to be victims of a scam because their money isn't stolen by a criminal with a gun or knife. Fraud victims are often very (**5**) <u>gullible</u> people. It's possible to (**6**) <u>swindle</u> them because they trust people too easily.

In a crime of fraud, the victim gives his or her money willingly, thinking that he or she will get something good in return. The (**7**) <u>con artists</u>, or criminals, don't tell the truth. They do anything to convince you to send your money. They act in a friendly manner to gain your trust. They (**8**) <u>reassure</u> you that they are telling the truth. They (**9**) <u>put pressure on</u> you to make a quick decision and send them money right away. The best way to (**10**) <u>protect yourself</u> against a scam is to check carefully before you send money to a company you don't know. If you are worried about a letter like this, throw it away. Don't become a victim of fraud!

_____ **a.** Ready to believe what people say (easily tricked)

_____ **b.** To believe someone is honest or something is true

_____ **c.** Something that you win in a contest

_____ **d.** To get money from someone by tricking him or her

_____ **e.** To try to make someone do something

     f. People who are hurt by someone or something

     g. Prevent yourself from being hurt

     h. People who trick others in order to get money from them

     i. To make someone feel calm and less worried

     j. Money that you pay now so that something won't be sold to another person

2 Focus on Listening

A LISTENING ONE: *Too Good to Be True*

 Listen to the beginning of the news report. Complete the items below. Discuss your answers with the class.

1. Match each person in the news report with the correct description. Write the letter in the blank.

     1. Nadine Chow   **a.** con artist

     2. Suzanne Markham   **b.** news reporter

     3. Frank Richland   **c.** victim

2. What do you think is going to happen to Suzanne?

LISTENING FOR MAIN IDEAS

Now listen to the whole report. Number the steps below to indicate the order in which they occur.

Steps in Telemarketing Fraud

The con artist . . .

     explains what will happen after winning.

     tells the victim about the deposit.

     puts pressure on the victim.

     reassures the victim the he's telling the truth.

     _1_ tells the victim about the prize.

LISTENING FOR DETAILS

Listen to the news report again. Circle the best answer to complete each sentence.

1. REPORTER: In the United States alone, people lose about _____ each year through telephone fraud.

   a. $4 billion   **b.** $14 billion   **c.** $40 billion

2. CON ARTIST: Ma'am, are you ready for _____ ?

   a. a free prize   **b.** another try   **c.** a big surprise

3. CON ARTIST: You've done it! You're our lucky winner! You've just won a luxury _____!

   a. vacation   **b.** car   **c.** home

4. REPORTER: He's using one of the _____—telling the victim she has just won a big prize.

   a. oldest stories   **b.** most common scams   **c.** biggest lies

5. CON ARTIST: As soon as we finish the paperwork, I'm going to _____.

   a. mail the ticket to your house   **b.** take your picture   **c.** call the hotel and airline

6. REPORTER: The con artist has done the first half of his job. Suzanne is _____ about winning a prize.

   a. puzzled   **b.** excited   **c.** happy

7. CON ARTIST: It's just _____.

   a. $100   **b.** $500   **c.** $5,000

8. REPORTER: To get the money, the con artist has to _____ her that he is telling the truth.

   a. trust   **b.** tell   **c.** reassure

9. REPORTER: After he feels that the victim trusts him, the con artist puts pressure on the victim to _____.

   a. make a quick decision   **b.** talk to her husband   **c.** call him back right away

10. REPORTER: You might think that Suzanne is more _____ than most, but the truth is, anyone can be a victim of fraud.

   a. gullible   **b.** stupid   **c.** unsure

REACTING TO THE LISTENING

 1 Listen to Suzanne's words and tone of voice in each excerpt. Choose one or two of the adjectives below to describe Suzanne's feelings. Write the adjective(s) in the column "Suzanne's Feelings." Then write the reason for your choice. Discuss your answers in small groups.

Adjectives to Describe Feelings

angry	excited	joyful	scared	unsure
cheerful	frustrated	pleased	surprised	worried
confident	happy	reassured		

	SUZANNE'S FEELINGS	REASON FOR YOUR CHOICE
Excerpt 1		
Excerpt 2		
Excerpt 3		
Excerpt 4		

2 Discuss the following questions with the class.

1. Why was Suzanne so easily swindled?

2. Some people become fraud victims more easily than others. For example, elderly people and tourists are often the victims of scams. Why are some people more gullible than others?

3. Could Frank Richland swindle you? How gullible are you?

B **LISTENING TWO:** *Interviews*

When we hear a story about telemarketing fraud, we often wonder how someone can trust a con artist.

 Listen to the interviews with other people whom Frank called. Match each victim with his or her reason for trusting Frank. Write the letter in the blank. One of the reasons does not match any of the interviewees.

Joe L.

Rosa A.

Peter S.

Beth G.

Victims

_____ **1.** Joe L. (age 65)

_____ **2.** Rosa A. (age 82)

_____ **3.** Peter S. (age 45)

_____ **4.** Beth G. (age 30)

Reasons for Trusting Frank

a. The victim didn't have any extra money.

b. The victim was lonely and liked talking to Frank.

c. Frank put pressure on the victim to make a quick decision.

d. The victim trusts people easily.

e. The victim had never heard of telephone fraud.

C **LINKING LISTENINGS ONE AND TWO**

Discuss these questions in small groups or as a whole class.

1. Each of the victims in Listening Two had a different reason for believing Frank. Which reason (or reasons) explains why Suzanne believed the con artist? Explain your choice.

2. Look at the names of fraud victims from Listenings One and Two in the chart on page 45. Who do you think is more likely* to be swindled again? Who do you think is less likely? Check the column in the chart that expresses your opinion. Then write a reason for your opinion.

---

more likely: has a greater possibility

Fraud victim	More likely to be swindled again	Less likely to be swindled again	Reason for your opinion
Suzanne M.			
Joe L.			
Rosa A.			
Peter S.			
Beth G.			

3 Focus on Vocabulary

1 *Read the sentences. Write each word in the correct blank.*

1. **con artist / victim**

   When the _____ realized that the _____ had stolen her money, she called the police.

2. **sweepstakes / prize**

   My sister bought a ticket for the _____ because she heard that the _____ was a trip to Hong Kong.

3. **crime / criminals**

   The _____ went to jail for their _____.

4. **protect / put pressure on**

   If you want to _____ yourself from scams, you shouldn't let anyone _____ you to buy something over the phone.

5. **trusted / reassured**

   Suzanne _____ Frank after he _____ her that she would get her prize in seven days.

6. payment / deposit

When you give a _____, you don't give the full _____.

7. scam / trick

In a telemarketing _____, the telemarketer tries to _____ you into sending money.

8. excited / gullible

Suzanne has always been _____. That's why she quickly became _____ when she heard about the Hawaii vacation.

9. rob / swindle

If a criminal tries to _____ you, it's an obvious crime. But if someone tries to _____ you, you might not realize that you are being hurt.

10. theft / fraud

_____ is a kind of _____ in which the criminal gets your money by telling you a lie.

2 *Work with a partner. Take turns describing your experiences with one or more of the situations listed below. As you tell your stories, use at least three words from the vocabulary box.*

You can begin your story like this:

A: I'd like to tell you about the time when . . .

B: What happened?

Situations

You (or someone you know):

- felt someone put pressure on you.
- protected yourself against a crime.
- were a victim of a scam.
- were gullible and believed someone who told you a lie.
- reassured someone who was in trouble.
- won a prize.

Vocabulary

Nouns	Verbs	Adjectives
con artist	cheat	angry
crime	lose	excited
deposit	pay	frustrated
fraud	protect	gullible
prize	put pressure on	happy
scam	reassure	luxury
sweepstakes	swindle	reassured
telemarketing	trick	unsure
victim	trust	worried

4 Focus on Speaking

A   PRONUNCIATION: Reductions

In speaking, some words are reduced. If a word is reduced, it joins with the previous word and the sounds of both words change. Reduced words are never stressed words.

Written English	Spoken English*
I **have to** pay a deposit. She **has to** pay a deposit.	I **hafta** pay a deposit. /hæftə/ She **hasta** pay a deposit. /hæstə/
I'm **going to** mail the ticket to your house. I'm **going to** the post office.	I'm **gonna** mail the ticket to your house. /gənə/ (**Going to** can be reduced because it is not the main verb in the sentence. In this sentence *mail* is the main verb.) BUT ~~I'm **gonna** the post office.~~ (**Going to** *cannot* be reduced because it is the main verb in the sentence and is stressed.)
I **want to** win a prize. She **wants to** win a prize.	I **wanna** win a prize. /wanə/ BUT ~~She **wanna** win a prize.~~ (The third person form **he / she wants to** cannot be reduced to **wanna**.) I **wanna** ~~to~~ win a prize (If you say **wanna**, do not add **to**.)

* **Note:** The boldfaced words in this column are written according to how they sound, not how they are spelled.

1   *Listen to the following pronunciation chant. Snap your fingers to the rhythm. Pay attention to the pronunciation of the reductions.*

CON ARTIST: Do you **wanna** get a prize?

Do you **wanna** get a prize?

VICTIM: Yes, I **wanna** get a prize.

Yes, I **wanna** get a prize.

CON ARTIST: First you **hafta** send the money.

First you **hafta** send the money.

VICTIM: I don't **wanna** send the money.

I don't **wanna** send the money.

CON ARTIST: You **hafta** send it now.

You **hafta** send it now.

VICTIM: I'm **gonna** call the cops.

I'm **gonna** call the cops.

As a class, listen and repeat as your teacher says the chant.

Next, say the chant in pairs. One student is the con artist. The other student is the victim. Remember to reduce the boldfaced words. Switch roles and repeat the chant.

Now work in two groups. One group is the con artist. The other group is the victim. Say the chant once. Then switch roles and repeat it.

2   *Read the following dialogue silently. Underline the verbs or phrases that can be reduced when the dialogue is spoken. Discuss your choices with the class.*

A: Hello, ma'am? Congratulations! You're going to be rich! I have an exciting prize for you.

B: Really? What do I have to do?

A: Well, first I have to ask you this. Which prize do you want to get: the luxury car or $10,000?

B: I want to get a new car, but I'd also like some money. Can I have both?

A: No, I'm sorry. You have to choose one.

B: Hold on. I'm going to ask my husband what he wants! . . . OK, I'm back. He says he wants to have the money. He has to pay a bunch of bills.

A: Great! Now, to get the prize, you have to send a small deposit of $500.

B: OK. Can you hang on? I'm going to get my checkbook.

Work with a partner to read the dialogue. Then switch roles and repeat. Use the correct reductions.

B | STYLE: Expressing and Asking for Opinions

People usually have strong opinions about fraud. You can express your opinions and ask for your classmates' opinions by using these expressions.

Expressing Your Opinion	Asking for an Opinion
I (don't) think (that) . . .	What do you think, (name)?
I (don't) believe (that) . . .	Do you agree, (name)?
In my opinion, . . .	How about you, (name)?
	What's your opinion about this, (name)?

1 *Read the group discussion below. Fill in each blank with an appropriate phrase from the box above. (There is more than one correct answer.)*

LEADER: (1) _____ you should never give your credit card number over the phone. You don't know who is on the other end. (2) _____, Soo-Mi?

SOO-MI: I disagree. (3) _____ it's OK to buy things that way if you are careful. Sometimes it's more convenient to use your credit card over the phone.

LEADER: (4) _____, Maria?

MARIA: I agree with Soo-Mi. (5) _____ that the most important thing is not to be gullible.

2 Now have a discussion like the one presented in Exercise 1. Work in groups of three or four students. Choose a discussion leader. The leader chooses one of the four statements below, reads it aloud, states an opinion, and explains it. Then the leader asks each person for an opinion.

Each student takes a turn leading a discussion. Each leader should choose a different statement to discuss.

Statements for Discussion

1. Victims of telemarketing fraud are not very intelligent.

2. Telemarketing fraud is a more serious crime than shoplifting.*

3. Telephone con artists should go to jail for a long time.

4. People should always report telemarketing fraud to the police.

C   GRAMMAR: Equatives and Comparatives

1 Read the following conversation, in which two people compare fraud with other kinds of crime. Notice the equatives (words that talk about things that are equal) and the comparatives (words that talk about more or less). Then answer the questions below.

A: Yesterday a woman stole $50 from me. She tricked me. She said the money would help a sick girl in the hospital.

B: What a scam! It's *worse than* being robbed by someone with a gun.

A: Well, I disagree. It's *not as dangerous as* being robbed.

B: Yes, but in the future you'll be *less trusting than* you were before.

A: That's true. I guess fraud is just *as bad as* other types of crime.

Discussion Questions

1. Which of the phrases expresses the idea that two things are *equal*?

2. Which of the phrases expresses the idea of *more*?

3. Which two of the phrases expresses the idea of *less*?

---

shoplifting: taking things from stores without paying

Equatives and Comparatives	Examples
Use **equatives** to express the idea of equal: • Use *as* + **adjective** + *as*.	Con artists are **as dishonest as** other criminals. (Con artists and other criminals are equally dishonest.)
Use **comparatives** to express the idea of more: • Use **adjective** + *-er* + *than* with one-syllable adjectives. • If an adjective ends in *-y*, change the *-y* to *-i* and add *-er* + *than*. • Use *more* + **adjective** + *than* with adjectives that have two or more syllables.	Con artists are **smarter than** their victims. Violent criminals are **scarier than** con artists. Telemarketing fraud is **more common than** medical fraud.
Use **comparatives** to express the idea of less: • Use *less* + **adjective** + *than*. • Use *not as* + **adjective** + *as*.	Medical fraud is **less common than** telemarketing fraud. Con artists **are not as dangerous as** violent criminals.
There are some irregular **comparative** forms.	**Adjective** **Comparative** *bad* *worse* *good* *better*

2 *Work with a partner. Student A gives an opinion (see Section 4B) and uses a comparison. Student B listens, agrees or disagrees, and tells why. Use the sentences on page 52. Switch roles after item 4.*

Example: _____ con artists are (dangerous) violent criminals.

STUDENT A: *I don't think that* con artists are <u>as dangerous as</u> violent criminals.

STUDENT B: *I agree because* violent criminals usually carry weapons and con artists don't.

1. _____ elderly people are (gullible) young people.

2. _____ medical fraud is (common) telemarketing fraud.

3. _____ tourists are (easy to swindle) locals.*

4. _____ criminal telemarketers are (dishonest) other kinds of con artists.

5. _____ con artists are (hard to catch) robbers.

6. _____ luxury hotel rooms are often (nice) they look in pictures.

7. _____ a victim of a scam is often (embarrassed) a victim of a robbery.

8. _____ a violent crime is (bad) a crime of fraud.

D ▌ SPEAKING TOPIC

There are many kinds of dishonest activities. Some are more serious than others. Work in small groups to evaluate different dishonest actions.

Step 1: As a group, discuss the dishonest actions and punishments listed. Next to each action, write the letter of the punishment that your group thinks is most appropriate. As you compare the actions and punishments, remember to use language for giving opinions and comparing (see Sections 4B and 4C).

Example: STUDENT A: *I think that* the punishment for selling something that you know will break should be "Go to jail."

STUDENT B: Really? *I think* it should be "Pay a fine." Jail is for *more serious* crimes, like "Taking money out of someone else's bank account. *That's worse.*"

Dishonest Actions

_____ 1. Lying about your work experience in order to get a job

_____ 2. Pretending that you are busy so that you don't have to attend a boring office party

_____ 3. Pretending to be poor so that the government will give you money

_____ 4. Lying about your health so that you don't have to go into the army

_____ 5. Taking money out of someone else's bank account

---

locals: people who are not visitors

------ 6. Telling someone to send you money for a prize that doesn't exist

------ 7. Finding a wallet with money and identification in it and not returning it to the owner

------ 8. Not saying anything if a store clerk gives you too much change by mistake

------ 9. Cheating on a test

------ 10. Selling something you know will break soon

Punishments

a. Go to jail

b. Lose your job/school position

c. Pay a fine (money)

d. No punishment

e. Other (explain):

_____

_____

_____

Step 2: Present your group's opinions to the class. Be prepared to give reasons for your choices.

E   RESEARCH TOPICS

WATCH A MOVIE

Step 1: Many movies tell stories about fraud, including *Green Card, Crouching Tiger/Hidden Dragon, The Thomas Crowne Affair, The Talented Mr. Ripley,* and *Working Girl.* With your class, watch a movie that deals with fraud. (You can go to a movie theater together or watch a video in class.)

Step 2: Meet in small groups and discuss the following questions.

1. What is this movie about? (Summarize it in one or two sentences.)

2. Who was tricked?

3. How did the person(s) get tricked?

4. Was anyone hurt because of the fraud? Why or why not?

5. Have you heard of a scam similar to the one in the movie? If so, what happened?

Step 3: Report to the class on your discussion.

RESEARCH ON FRAUD

Step 1: Choose a type of fraud to research. Select from identity theft, sweepstakes scams, medical fraud, Internet fraud, telemarketing scams, or another type of fraud of your choosing.

Step 2: Go to the library and look up your topic in an encyclopedia or on the Internet. Use the following questions to help you with your research.

- How does the fraud work? What does the con artist do?
- Who are usually the victims of this type of fraud? How much money do they lose?
- How can you protect yourself?

Step 3: Make a poster presenting information about the fraudulent activity. You can set it up like the one below or choose a different format.

MAGAZINE SUBSCRIPTION FRAUD

HOW IT WORKS: You buy magazine subscriptions.
The con artist promises a prize.
You never receive the magazine or the prize.

WHO THE VICTIMS ARE: 60% elderly people

HOW TO PROTECT YOURSELF:

1. Don't buy magazine subscriptions over the phone.
2. Find out the real price of a magazine subscription.
3. Don't buy magazines in order to get a big prize.

Step 4: Show the poster to your class and explain the fraud in detail.

Listening Task

As you listen, note how the types of fraud are similar or different. After the presentations, work as a class to make a list of general rules to protect yourselves from all types of fraud.

For Unit 3 Internet activities, visit the NorthStar Companion Website at
http://www.longman.com/northstar.

The Art of Storytelling

1 Focus on the Topic

A PREDICTING

Discuss these questions with the class.

1. What's happening in the photo?

2. Read the title of the unit. Why is storytelling an art? How is it similar to the art of painting or dancing?

B   SHARING INFORMATION

Discuss these questions with a partner.

1. Did anyone tell you stories when you were a child? Who told the stories? What kind of stories did you hear?

2. People have told stories for thousands of years as a form of entertainment. Today we can also read stories in books or watch them in movies or on TV. What do you like about each type of entertainment? Write your opinions.

   a. Listening to someone tell a story: _____

   _____

   b. Reading a book: _____

   _____

   c. Seeing a movie: _____

   _____

3. Which type of storytelling entertainment do you like best? Why? Share your answers with the class.

C   PREPARING TO LISTEN

BACKGROUND

Read the biography of storyteller Jackie Torrence on page 57. Then discuss the following questions with the class.

1. What things did Jackie Torrence do as a child to help prepare her for a career in storytelling?

2. What problems has Jackie overcome in her life?

3. Look at the photo of Jackie. How do her face and body language help to make her a good storyteller?

THE BIRTH OF A
STORYTELLER

Jackie Torrence spent her childhood in North Carolina, in the southern part of the United States. She was a shy child because she had problems with her teeth, which made it hard for her to talk. Other children teased her because of her speech problem, so she spent much of her childhood playing alone. One of Jackie's favorite games was to pretend she was on television. She told stories out loud using gestures and dramatic voices. At school, Jackie soon learned that she was good at writing stories, and with the help of her favorite teacher, she started to work on improving her speech.

Jackie Torrence, storyteller

Jackie's first storytelling performance was in a library. She was working as a librarian and was asked to entertain a group of children. Jackie told them a story and they loved it! Before long, she began telling stories within her community. Many of her stories came from old American and African-American folktales. Eventually, she started telling stories across North America.

As Jackie's fame increased, her health decreased. She now has to use a wheelchair, but this has not stopped her storytelling career. Jackie's stories have been published in books, magazines, and newspapers and she has appeared on radio and television. She has won awards for nine of her sound recordings and three of her television specials.

VOCABULARY FOR COMPREHENSION

1 *Match each underlined word with a definition or synonym listed below. Write the correct letter in the blank.*

a. purple

b. progressed slowly

c. moved closer to

d. cold

e. shone on

f. partner

g. party

h. demanding that rules be obeyed

_____ **1.** Clara and her friends went to the spring <u>social</u>. It was a dinner and dance in the town hall.

_____ **2.** She didn't have a <u>date</u> for the dance so she went alone.

_____ **3.** As she <u>approached</u> the town hall, she could see that it was full of people.

_____ **4.** The plants were covered with light-colored flowers: pink, yellow, and <u>lavender</u>.

_____ **5.** As the night <u>wore on</u>, Clara became tired from dancing. It was late, so she decided to go home.

_____ **6.** Also, Clara's parents were a little <u>strict</u>, so they told her to come home early.

_____ **7.** The light from the moon <u>fell on</u> her hair and her long dress.

_____ **8.** When she arrived home, Clara felt <u>chilled</u>. She was happy to go inside and get warm.

2 *Look at the picture on page 59. Write the letter next to the corresponding word. Consult a dictionary if necessary.*

_____ **1.** cemetery   _____ **4.** headlights

_____ **2.** driveway   _____ **5.** picket fence

_____ **3.** gravestone   _____ **6.** weeds

2 Focus on Listening

A   LISTENING ONE: "Lavender"

Listen to the beginning of the story "Lavender." What do you think will happen to Robert and David?

1. They will meet someone.
2. They will see something strange.
3. They will get lost.

LISTENING FOR MAIN IDEAS

 Listen to the story. Write answers to the questions. You do not need to write full sentences. Discuss your answers with the class.

1. Robert and David go to a spring social. Who do they meet while driving down the highway?

   _____

2. What does Robert give to Lavender at the dance?

   _____

3. Where do Robert and David take Lavender after the dance?

   _____

4. Where do Robert and David go the next day?

   _____

5. What do Robert and David discover about Lavender at the end of the story?

   _____

LISTENING FOR DETAILS

 *Listen again. Put the events from the story in order. Write **1** next to the event that happened first, **2** next to the second event, and so on.*

_____ a. Robert and David saw a girl wearing a lavender evening dress.

_____ b. They noticed that the windows on the house were broken.

_____ c. Robert and David realized that they didn't have dates for the evening.

_____ d. Weeds and grass had grown up in Lavender's driveway.

_____ e. The name on the gravestone was "Lavender."

_____ f. Lavender said that her parents were a little strict.

_____ g. Robert and David danced with Lavender.

Compare your answers with a partner's. Discuss any differences with the class.

REACTING TO THE LISTENING

 1 *Listen to the following excerpts. Jackie Torrence uses changes in volume (loud/soft), speed (slow/fast), and pitch (high/low) to show Robert and David's emotions.*

On the chart below, circle the two adjectives that best describe the character's emotions at each point in the story. Then circle the techniques that Torrence uses. There may be more than one technique used in each excerpt.

	ADJECTIVES THAT DESCRIBE EMOTIONS	TECHNIQUES
Excerpt 1	Robert feels . . . **a.** in love **b.** shy **c.** sad	Jackie Torrence uses changes in . . . **a.** volume (loud/soft) **b.** speed (slow/fast) **c.** pitch (high/low)
Excerpt 2	Robert feels . . . **a.** angry **b.** confused **c.** worried	Jackie Torrence uses changes in . . . **a.** volume **b.** speed **c.** pitch
Excerpt 3	Robert and David feel . . . **a.** afraid **b.** lonely **c.** uncomfortable	Jackie Torrence uses changes in . . . **a.** volume **b.** speed **c.** pitch

2 *Discuss your answers in small groups. Explain why you chose certain adjectives. How do the techniques fit the emotions?*

3 *Work in small groups. Discuss these questions.*

1. When did you first think that something strange was happening in the story?

2. Were the characters believable? Why or why not?

3. Were you surprised by the ending? Why or why not?

B LISTENING TWO: *An Interview with Jackie Torrence*

1 *Listen to an interview with storyteller Jackie Torrence. She describes the steps she takes in learning to tell a new story. Listen for the first three steps and draw lines to match the step with the activity.*

Step	Activity
1. The first time, . . .	**a.** read the story for the words.
2. The second time, . . .	**b.** read the story for the pictures.
3. The third time, . . .	**c.** decide whether you like the story.

2 *What does Jackie Torrence mean by reading the story "for the words" and "for the pictures"? Share your ideas with the class.*

3 *In the interview, Jackie Torrence says, "You can make it [the story] or break it [the story] by saying the right or wrong words." What do you think she means by that?*

C LINKING LISTENINGS ONE AND TWO

Discuss the following questions with a partner. Present your answers during class discussion.

1. In the interview, Jackie Torrence says, "As you read about the characters, you read a personality into those characters." What is the personality of each character in the story? Write two or three adjectives to describe each character.

David

_____

_____

_____

Robert

_____

_____

_____

Lavender

_____

_____

_____

2. What can you tell about Jackie Torrence's personality from her storytelling and interview? Write three adjectives to describe Jackie's personality and share them with the class.

_____   _____   _____

3 Focus on Vocabulary

1 *Use the letters to make a word to complete each sentence.*

1. ETDA

   Do you have a _____*date*_____ for the dance?

2. RALVEEND

   Her dress was _____ and yellow.

3. ERWO NO

   As the night _____ _____, I became tired.

4. SCITRT

   My parents are _____ and won't let me go out at night.

5. LELF NO

   The light _____ _____ her face, and I could see that she was worried.

6. DELICHL

   I felt _____ in the cold air.

7. VEYIWDRA

   I drove up the _____ to the house.

8. SLEDHAGIHT

   The _____ of my car lit up the dark road.

9. KEPCIT CEEFN

   There was a white _____ _____ around the house.

10. ESWED

    The _____ had grown tall in the garden.

2 *Work with a partner. Look at the pictures to help retell the story of "Lavender." Take turns telling the story. Use the past tense and vocabulary you have learned in this unit.*

Picture 1

Picture 2

Picture 3

Picture 4

4 Focus on Speaking

A prepositional phrase consists of a preposition (P) and a noun phrase (NP).

Example: They drove <u>to</u> <u>the social</u>.

Rule	Example
Short prepositions: *to, at, in, of, on, with, for, from* are not stressed in prepositional phrases.	Lavender rode **in their car.** They danced **with Lavender.**
Unstressed prepositions join closely to the other words in a prepositional phrase. (In the example, the prepositional phrases and single words have the same stress.)	**for breakfast** forbidden **in the rain** unafraid
Some prepositions have reduced pronunciations: The vowel is pronounced /ə/ in speaking.	**at home** *at* is /ət/ **for dinner** *for* is /fər/; rhymes with *her* **to school** *to* is usually /tə/; sounds like t'school **in town** *in* is /ən/ or /ɪn/

1 Listen to the sentences below and on page 66. Complete the sentences with the prepositions you hear.

1. Robert and David drove _____ their house.

2. Lavender was waiting _____ the road.

3. She walked _____ Robert.

4. The three friends went _____ the dance.

5. They got back _____ the car.

6. Robert and David were looking _____ the coat in the backyard.

7. Robert pointed _____ the gravestone.

8. They ran _____ the car.

Compare your answers with a partner's. Take turns saying the sentences out loud. Try to use the /ə/ sound when appropriate.

2 *Read the following phrases aloud to yourself. Match each phrase in Column 1 to a phrase in Column 2 that has a similar stress pattern. Write the letters in the blanks.*

Column 1

_____ **1.** come to dinner

_____ **2.** Thanks for getting a job.

_____ **3.** It's hard to dance.

_____ **4.** a fortune at school

_____ **5.** at nine

_____ **6.** point at Tom

Column 2

a. a fortunate school

b. pointed top

c. It's cold today.

d. come tomorrow

e. Hank's forgetting his job.

f. arrive

 Listen to the answers. Did you match the columns correctly? Repeat the phrases after your teacher.

Work with a partner. Student A reads a phrase from Column 1. Student B reads the matching phrase in Column 2. Switch columns and repeat.

B   STYLE: Using Descriptive Language

Descriptive language creates images, or pictures, in our minds. Storytellers use descriptive language to help their listeners imagine the characters and situations in their stories. When Jackie Torrence said that the right or wrong words could make or break a story, she was talking about descriptive language.

Read the following sentence:

The car drove down the street.

There are several ways to make this sentence more descriptive:

Ways to Make Language Descriptive	Example Sentence
Use adjectives and adverbs.	The **old** car drove **slowly** down the street.
Add details.	The old **station wagon** drove slowly down **Main Street, the only road in town.**
Use words that appeal to the senses (sight, sound, touch, smell, taste).	The old station wagon **rattled** slowly down Main Street, the only road in town.

1 *Form groups of four and sit in a circle. Student A reads sentence 1 from the list below. Student B adds at least one adjective or adverb. Student C adds at least one detail (for example, a name or a personal detail). Student D adds at least one word that appeals to the senses. Write down Student D's sentence.*

Example: STUDENT A: The boy walked into the building. (sentence)

STUDENT B: The <u>little</u> boy walked into the building. (+ adjective)

STUDENT C: The little boy walked into the <u>police station</u>. (+ detail)

STUDENT D: The little boy walked into the <u>dark, cold</u> police station. (+ senses)

Repeat the activity with each sentence. Take turns being Student A, Student B, Student C, and Student D.

Sentences

1. The boy went to the store.
2. The woman drove into the parking lot.
3. I asked the man for directions.
4. The man opened the door.
5. We went to the movie.
6. The girl fell into the pool.
7. The bus went up the hill.
8. The two people went along the road.

2 *Share with the rest of the class three of the sentences that your group wrote. As you hear the sentences from other groups, listen for:*

1. The adjective that you think is the most descriptive

2. The detail that you think is the most interesting

3. The sensory word that you think is the most powerful

C   GRAMMAR: Infinitives of Purpose

1 *Read the following conversation among David, Robert, and their friend Mary. Notice the infinitives of purpose in italics.*

MARY: Why did you give a strange girl a ride in your car?

DAVID: It was so dark on the road. We stopped *to see* if she needed help.

MARY: Are you sure that's the only reason?

DAVID: Well . . . I guess we also stopped *in order to see* if she was going to the social.

MARY: So at the end of the evening, why did you drop her off at the end of the driveway instead of taking her up to the house?

ROBERT: Well, we did that *in order not to meet* her parents. She said they wouldn't approve of her riding with us.

MARY: Then why did you go back the next day?

ROBERT: *To get* the coat and *to see* her again.

Answer the following questions.

1. What word comes before the verb in an infinitive?

2. What form does the verb take in an infinitive?

3. Which one of the following questions does an infinitive of purpose answer: *Who? What? When? Why?* or *How?*

Infinitives of Purpose	Examples
To explain the purpose of an action: • Use an **infinitive**. • Use *in order* + **infinitive**.	We stopped **to see** if she needed help. We also stopped **in order to see** if she was going to the social.
To explain a negative purpose: • Use *in order not* + **infinitive**.	We did that **in order not to meet** her parents.
To answer the question *Why?* • Use an **infinitive**.	A: Why did you go back the next day? B: We wanted **to get** the coat and **to see** her again.

2 *Work with a partner. Match each action with the reason for the action. Write the letter in the blank.*

Action

___e___ **1.** David and Robert went to the social.

_____ **2.** On the way, David and Robert stopped on the road.

_____ **3.** After the social, David and Robert dropped Lavender off at the top of the driveway.

_____ **4.** David and Robert let Lavender keep the coat.

_____ **5.** The next day, David and Robert went back to the house.

Reason

a. They didn't want to make her parents angry.

b. They wanted to look for Lavender.

c. They wanted to see if Lavender needed a ride.

d. They wanted to have an excuse to see her again.

e. They wanted to have some fun.

For each match, combine the action and the reason into one sentence that contains an infinitive of purpose. Take turns saying the sentences. Listen to each other's sentences and correct any mistakes.

Example: STUDENT A: David and Robert went to the social to had some fun.

STUDENT B: I think it should be "to <u>have</u> some fun."

STUDENT A: Oh yeah! "David and Robert went to the social to have some fun."

3 *Keep the same partner from Exercise 2. Student A asks question 1 below. Student B answers, using an infinitive of purpose. Student A writes down Student B's answer. Switch roles after question 3. Then compare your answers with another pair's.*

1. Why did David and Robert stop the car on the way to the social?

2. Why did Robert give Lavender his coat?

3. Why did Lavender walk up the driveway by herself?

4. Why did Lavender blow a kiss to the young men?

5. Why did David and Robert go back to Lavender's house the next day?

6. Why did David and Robert walk to the back of the house?

D SPEAKING TOPIC

Write a continuation of the story "Lavender" and perform it for the class.

PREPARING

Work in groups of three or four to create your continuation. Use one of the sentences below to begin. Remember to use descriptive language (see Section 4B).

Sentence 1: Robert picked up his coat and saw the name "Lavender" on the gravestone. Then Robert and David . . .

Sentence 2: The next month, Robert and David went to another spring social. As they were driving down the highway . . .

Sentence 3: Twenty years later, Robert and David were again driving down the highway. They . . .

PRACTICING

As a group, read through the story twice. Each person should read part of the story. The first time, focus on fluency and pronunciation. The second time, focus on speaking with drama and emotion. Then practice the story as if it were a performance.

PERFORMING

Perform your story in front of the class.

E   RESEARCH TOPICS

LISTENING TO A STORY

Step 1:   Listen to a relative or friend tell a story. Tape-record your voice as you answer the following questions about the story.

- What is the name of the story?

- Who told it to you?

- Who are the main characters? Give a one-sentence description of each character.

- What happens in the story? Give a brief summary of the plot.

- Do you like this story? Why or why not?

Step 2:   Give the tape to your teacher for feedback.

DISCUSSING WELL-KNOWN STORIES

Step 1:   Meet in a small group. Think of a well-known story or folktale (for example, "Cinderella," "Little Red Riding Hood," "The Sun and the Moon").

Step 2:   On your own, interview two people (outside of class) about the story. Take notes on questions 3 and 4 as you listen.

Interview Questions

1. Do you know the story "_____"?

2. When did you first hear it?

3. Do you know any other versions of this story? What are the differences?

4. Why is this story so well known? (Give your opinion.)

5. _____ ? (Add a question.)

Step 3:   Meet with your group. Report on questions 3 and 4. Compare your answers with those of the group.

For Unit 4 Internet activities, visit the NorthStar Companion Website at http://www.longman.com/northstar.

Separated by the Same Language

1 Focus on the Topic

A PREDICTING

Discuss these questions with the class.

1. Look at the cartoon. Are the men talking about the same thing?

2. In what country do people say "queue"? In what country do they say "line"?

3. English novelist Sir Walter Besant (1836–1901) said: "England and America are two countries separated by the same language." What did he mean?

B SHARING INFORMATION

Write answers to these questions. Then discuss the questions in small groups.

1. When you hear a person speak in your native language, what can you tell from that person's accent? Check one or more boxes below.

   hometown   ❑
   economic class   ❑
   level of education   ❑
   profession   ❑
   age   ❑
   intelligence   ❑
   other: _____   ❑

2. Are some accents in your native language considered better than others? Why or why not?

C PREPARING TO LISTEN

BACKGROUND

1 *Read the excerpt from a textbook on linguistics (the study of language).*

Introduction to Linguistics: Dialect

A *dialect* is a form of a language with grammar, pronunciation, and vocabulary that differ from other forms of the language. A dialect develops when a group of same-language speakers are separated in some way.

Regional dialects develop when speakers are separated by geography, such as rivers and mountains.

Social dialects develop when one group is separated from another socially because of differences in economic class, culture, ethnicity, or age.

A *standard dialect* is the dialect that is usually used in the media (television, radio, and newspapers). It is taught in schools and described in dictionaries and grammar books.

2 *Match each type of dialect with an example. Write the letter in the blank. Discuss your answers with the class.*

Type of Dialect

_____ 1. Regional dialect

_____ 2. Social dialect

_____ 3. Standard dialect

Example

a. Castilian (a dialect of Spanish used in dictionaries and grammar books)

b. Cockney (a dialect of English spoken in the East End of London)

c. Black vernacular English (a dialect of English spoken by African-Americans)

3 *What are some dialects in your own language? Share your information with the class. Discuss whether the dialects are regional, social, or standard.*

VOCABULARY FOR COMPREHENSION

Circle the answer that best completes the definition of each underlined word.

1. When I moved to my new school, it took a while for the other kids to <u>accept</u> me and start being my friend.

   To <u>accept</u> someone means to let that person become _____.

   a. part of a group   **b.** the leader of a group

2. When I moved here, I <u>became aware</u> of my accent. I didn't think about it before.

   To <u>become aware</u> means to _____ something.

   a. suddenly know   **b.** try to stop

3. My brother is very <u>bright</u>. He is always the best student in his class.

   A <u>bright</u> person is _____.

   a. happy   **b.** intelligent

4. Maria has an unusual accent, and people always <u>comment on</u> it. They always say, "You have such an unusual accent!"

   To <u>comment on</u> something means to _____ about it.

   a. give an opinion   **b.** ask a question

5. As a teenager, I tried to <u>fit in</u> with the other kids. I tried to wear the same clothes and talk the same way.

   To <u>fit in</u> means to _____ others in a group.

   a. be more fashionable than   **b.** be similar to

6. For many people, their job is more than what they do for work. It forms their personality and becomes part of their <u>identity</u>.

   A person's <u>identity</u> is _____.

   a. who a person is   **b.** what a person feels

7. I left my door unlocked, but it wasn't a mistake. I did it <u>intentionally</u> so that I could get back in without my key.

When something is done <u>intentionally</u>, it is done _____.

   a. by accident   **b.** on purpose

8. Teenagers often use <u>slang</u> that adults don't use. For example, kids today say something is "da bomb" to mean something is "the best."

<u>Slang</u> is _____ used by people in a particular group.

   a. formal words   **b.** informal words

9. Many people feel <u>self-conscious</u> when they make a speech in front of a group. They are afraid of what the people in the audience will think of them.

Being <u>self-conscious</u> means being worried about what _____.

   a. you think of other people   **b.** other people think of you

10. People often <u>stereotype</u> me because I'm tall. They think I must be good at playing basketball.

To <u>stereotype</u> means to have ideas about what people are like because of how they _____.

   a. play sports   **b.** look or sound

2 Focus on Listening

A   LISTENING ONE: *Accent and Identity*

Lisa

Peter

Lisa is a graduate student in a linguistics class. She is doing a class project on how people feel about their accents. You will hear her interview Peter, a native English speaker.

Listen to the excerpt. Where do you think Peter is from? Circle the name of the country.

a. United States

d. Australia

b. England

e. South Africa

c. St. Lucia, West Indies

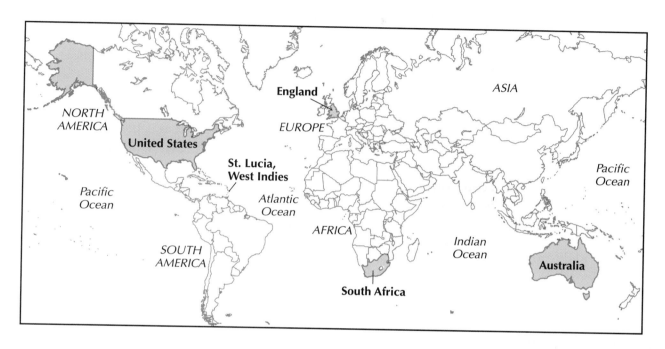

LISTENING FOR MAIN IDEAS

 Listen to an interview between Lisa and Peter. Circle the best answer to complete each sentence.

1. Before Peter came to the United States, he _____ his accent.
   a. felt self-conscious about
   b. wanted to preserve
   c. was not aware of

2. When Peter first came to the United States, he felt that he _____ because of his accent.
   a. didn't fit in
   b. couldn't communicate
   c. didn't meet people

3. Now Peter feels that his accent is _____.
   a. helpful in his work
   b. not as strong as before
   c. part of his identity

LISTENING FOR DETAILS

 Listen to the interview again. Circle the answers.

1. Peter grew up in _____.
   a. England   b. St. Lucia   c. Australia

2. Peter felt that some people thought he was not _____ because he talked slowly.
   a. friendly   b. honest   c. intelligent

3. Peter got tired of explaining his _____ to people he met.
   a. opinions   b. culture   c. background

4. Peter tried to change his accent so that he could fit in _____.
   a. at college   b. at work   c. at home

5. Peter liked living at International House because everyone _____.
   a. accepted his accent   b. spoke another language   c. tried to change their accent

6. Now Peter speaks with _____.
   a. an American accent   b. a West Indian accent   c. no accent

REACTING TO THE LISTENING

 1 *Listen to the excerpts about different times in Peter's life. Rate how positive or negative Peter felt during each time period. Circle a number from –2 (most negative) to +2 (most positive). Then write down some key words that show how he felt. Share your answers with the class.*

	Negative			Positive	

Excerpt 1: In St. Lucia

How did Peter feel about his accent?	–2	–1	0	+1	+2
How did Peter feel about himself?	–2	–1	0	+1	+2

Key words: _____

Excerpt 2: During college

How did Peter feel about his accent?	–2	–1	0	+1	+2
How did Peter feel about himself?	–2	–1	0	+1	+2

Key words: _____

Excerpt 3: Now

How does Peter feel about his accent?	–2	–1	0	+1	+2
How does Peter feel about himself?	–2	–1	0	+1	+2

Key words: _____

2 *Discuss these questions in small groups.*

1. Do you think it is polite to ask people about their accents? Why or why not?

2. For several years, Peter felt self-conscious about his accent. Would you feel the same way? Why or why not? What would you do?

3. Peter says that a person's accent is part of his or her identity. Do you agree? Explain why or why not.

B   LISTENING TWO: *Code Switching*

 You will hear a lecture on code switching. *In linguistics, the word* code *is used to mean* language *or* dialect. *Fill in the missing definitions and examples in the lecture notes below.*

LINGUISTICS

→ more on <u>dialect</u>

Code switching = changing _____

    Ex: One dialect at _____

       Another dialect at _____

Teenage dialect (slang)

"Gotta bounce. Me & the crew are going shopping for some phat gear."

    Gotta bounce = _____

    the crew = _____

    phat gear = _____

Teens speak differently because _____

_____

_____

C   LINKING LISTENINGS ONE AND TWO

Discuss the questions in pairs or small groups. Then share your ideas with the class.

1. Does Peter speak a regional dialect or a social dialect? What about the teenagers described in Listening Two?

2. Decide whether Peter and an American teenager would agree with these statements about the way they speak. Read the statements and write *Yes* or *No*.

STATEMENT	PETER	AMERICAN TEENAGER
People always comment on the way I speak.		
I speak differently from the way people around me speak.		
I want to change the way I speak.		
Other people don't like the way I speak.		
The way I speak is part of my identity.		

3. In what ways might Peter and an American teenager feel the same? In what ways might they feel different?

3 Focus on Vocabulary

1 *Read the paragraphs about Peter. Complete the sentences with words from the list below. Discuss your answers with a partner.*

accepted	bright	fit in	intentionally	slang
became aware	commented on	identity	self-conscious	stereotyped

After coming to the United States, Peter (1) _____ that he had an accent. He noticed his accent because many people (2) _____ it. The comments made him feel (3) _____. He knew that some people (4) _____ him because of the way he spoke. He could tell that they thought he wasn't very (5) _____ because he talked slowly.

In college, Peter wanted to (6) _____ with the other students. He tried to speak like his friends by using (7) _____ when he talked. Also, as he spent more time with Americans, his accent began to change. He didn't change his accent (8) _____. It just happened naturally. Luckily, during his college years, Peter had friends at International House who (9) _____ his accent. They liked him for who he was, not how he talked.

Now Peter still has a slight accent, but he feels that his accent is part of his (10) _____. He is comfortable with who he is.

2 *This game of Truth or Dare** *will help you to review vocabulary from this unit and learn more about your classmates.*

1. Play in groups of five or six. Sit in a circle. In each turn, two people play: A Questioner asks questions, and a Player answers the questions or accepts a dare.

2. Choose the first person to be the Questioner. The Questioner plays with the person on his or her left.

3. The Questioner asks the Player, "Truth or Dare?"

4a. If the Player says "Truth": The Questioner asks the Player a question from the list below and on page 82. The Player must answer the question truthfully. The Questioner can ask follow-up questions to get more information.

4b. If the Player says "Dare": The Questioner chooses a dare from the list on page 82. The Questioner also chooses a word from the box below the dares. The Player must use that word in his or her response to the dare.

5. When the turn is finished, the Player becomes the next Questioner. The game continues until everyone in the group has had a turn.

"Truth" Questions

1. What makes you feel *self-conscious*? Why?

2. Have you ever *stereotyped* someone? Why?

3. Have you ever been *stereotyped*? How?

4. What is the most important part of your *identity*? Why?

5. What is the *brightest* thing you have ever done?

**dare:* to challenge someone to do something that is difficult or embarrassing

6. Have you ever *intentionally* hurt someone's feelings? Why?

7. What is the strangest thing you have ever done to *fit in* with a group of friends?

8. Do you *accept* most people the way they are, or are some things unacceptable to you? Give an example.

9. What kind of *slang* do you use with your friends? Give an example in English or your native language.

10. Do you speak or understand more than one *dialect* in your native language? If not, why not? If so, do you *code-switch*?

"Dares"

1. Without speaking, act out the meaning of the word.

2. Sing a short song using the word.

3. Spell the word without looking at it.

4. Spell the word backward without looking at it.

5. Use the word in a sentence about yourself.

6. Say another word or phrase that has a similar meaning.

7. Use the word in a sentence about someone else in the class.

8. Say a word or phrase that has the opposite meaning of the word.

accent	code switching	identity	slang
accept	comment on	intentionally	social
aware	dialect	regional	standard
bright	fit in	self-conscious	stereotype

4 Focus on Speaking

A PRONUNCIATION: *Can / Can't*

It is sometimes difficult for students to hear and pronounce the difference between *can* and *can't*. Native speakers don't listen for the /t/ sound in *can't*. Instead, they listen for the length of the sound of the letter *a*.

Listen to the example:

STUDENT A: Can you speak any foreign languages?

STUDENT B: Yes, I can. I can speak Chinese. But I can't speak very fluently yet. How about you?

STUDENT A: I can read French, but I can't speak it very well.

What differences did you hear in the spoken pronunciation of *can* and *can't*?

Can/Can't	Examples
Can is not stressed in most sentences and questions. It is pronounced /kən/, with a short unclear vowel.	"I **can** /kən/ speak Chinese." "I **can** /kən/ read French."
Can is stressed when it ends a sentence or clause.	"Yes, I **can** /kæn/." "If I **can** /kæn/, I will take a Chinese class."
Can't is always stressed. The vowel sound in *can't* is /æ/, like the vowel in *hand*.	"I **can't** /kænt/ speak it very fluently yet." "I **can't** /kænt/ take that Chinese class."

 1 *Listen to the following sentences. Circle* **can** *or* **can't.** *Compare your answers with a partner's.*

1. She *can/can't* take that class.

2. He *can/can't* speak French.

3. I *can/can't* understand American slang.

4. We *can/can't* speak that dialect.

5. I *can/can't* recognize his accent.

6. She *can/can't* fit in.

7. I *can/can't* comment on that.

8. She invited me to come. I said that I *can/can't*.

2 *Work in pairs to practice pronouncing* **can** *and* **can't.**

Student A reads each sentence below to Student B, using either **can** *or* **can't,** *with the correct pronunciation.*

Student B listens to the sentences. If he or she hears **can** */kən/ or /kæn/, Student B says "So can /kən/ I." If he or she hears* **can't** */kænt/, Student B says "Neither can /kən/ I." After Student A completes all the sentences, switch roles.*

1. She *can/can't* take that class.

2. He *can/can't* speak French.

3. I *can/can't* understand American slang.

4. We *can/can't* speak that dialect.

5. I *can/can't* recognize his accent.

6. She *can/can't* fit in.

7. I *can/can't* comment on that.

8. She invited me to come. I said that I *can/can't.*

B   STYLE: Leading a Small-Group Discussion

In a group discussion, it is useful to have a leader who helps control and direct the conversation. The leader must know how to start and end the discussion, how to keep the discussion on the topic, and what to do if someone doesn't talk or talks too much.

1 *Read the phrases that you can use to lead a discussion. (Don't fill in the blanks or check the boxes. They will be used for a later activity.)*

Starting a Discussion

❏ Let's talk about . . .

❏ Today I'd like to discuss . . .

_____

_____

Getting Everyone to Speak

a. Asking someone to talk

❏ What do you think, (name)?

❏ (name), do you agree?

_____

_____

b. Asking someone to stop talking

❑ That's a good point, (name). Can we hear from someone else?

❑ I see your point, (name). Does anyone agree or disagree?

_____

_____

Staying on the Topic

❑ Let's get back to our discussion about . . .

❑ I'd like to return to the topic. What do you think about . . . ?

_____

_____

Ending a Discussion

❑ That's all we have time for today.

❑ To sum up . . . (You summarize the ideas expressed in the discussion.)

_____

_____

2 *Work in groups of four students. Choose one student to be the discussion leader and one student to be the observer. The discussion leader chooses one of the questions from the list below and leads a five-minute discussion. The observer follows these instructions:*

1. Listen quietly, looking at the list on page 84 and above and checking off the phrases you hear.

2. Write any additional words or phrases the discussion leader uses in the blanks.

3. Show the completed checklist to the discussion leader.

Each member of the group should have a turn as both the discussion leader and the observer.

Discussion Questions

1. Should teenagers be allowed to use slang in school? Why or why not?

2. Should someone with a regional accent try to change it when he or she moves to a new place? Why or why not?

3. What is the best way to improve your accent when you speak English?

4. What is the best age for learning a foreign language? Why?

C   GRAMMAR: Modals of Ability and Possibility

1 *Read the paragraph. Underline the modals **can, can't, could,** and **couldn't.** Then discuss the questions below with the class.*

> I have learned many things this year in English class. When I started this class, I could only say "hello" and "goodbye." I couldn't have a conversation. However, I have learned a lot since then. I still can't explain everything I'm thinking, but I can talk to my friends and understand my classes. Hopefully, I can take another English class next semester, so my English will keep improving. I could also try to make more English-speaking friends.

1. Which sentences above are about past events?

2. Which are about the present?

3. Which are about the future?

Modals of Ability and Possibility	Examples
The modals *can* and *could* are followed by the base form of the verb.	I **can do** that. **Could** you **hear** me?
Can expresses ability in the present. *Can't* is the negative of *can*.	She **can** speak English. He **can't** speak French.
Could expresses ability in the past. *Couldn't* is the negative of *could*.	Last year, I **could** say a few words in English. I **couldn't** have a conversation in English last year.
Can and *could* also express possibility in the future.	Next year, you **can** study French. He **could** study more next time.

2 *Work in a pairs. Discuss how much your English has improved in the past year. Using the list below, take turns asking and answering questions about what you could and couldn't do in English a year ago and what you can and can't do in English now. Then think of other things that are not on the list.*

Could/Can you . . . ?

1. understand a movie

2. make small talk

3. order food in a restaurant

4. discuss philosophy

5. talk on the telephone

6. speak without an accent

7. _____

8. _____

3 *What can you do in the future to improve your English? Make a list of possible things using* can *and* could.

Example

I can take another class.

I could watch more movies in English.

Share your list with a partner. Report to the class any similarities.

Example

We hope we can join a conversation group.

We both thought we could take another class.

D   SPEAKING TOPIC

Work in small groups of three or four students. You will each lead a group discussion.

Step 1:   Each student chooses a different situation from the following list.

Situation 1

Mike is a TV news reporter from the state of Mississippi. He is applying for a job as reporter on a national news program that will be seen all over the United States. Mike speaks with a southern accent, not the standard American accent of many other reporters. Mike is worried that he will not get the job because of his accent. What should Mike do?

Situation 2

Judy is a high school student. She grew up in England and just moved to Australia. She feels self-conscious at school because her accent is different. She wants to fit in but she feels silly speaking with an Australian accent because she doesn't do it very well. What should Judy do?

Situation 3

Angelique works as a salesperson in a French clothing store in the United States. She speaks fluent English with a French accent. Her boss likes the way she speaks. He thinks her accent helps sell clothing. Her friends like the way she speaks. They say her accent makes her different and special. Angelique has recently become an American citizen. She thinks she should change her accent to sound more American. What should Angelique do?

Situation 4

Sharon works for a financial company in a small city in the United States. She recently hired Meir, who speaks English very well though he was not born in the United States. Sharon is happy with Meir's work. However, there are problems between Meir and some people on her staff. These people are frustrated because they have a difficult time understanding Meir because of his accent. What should Sharon do?

Step 2: Beginning with the student who chose Situation 1, take turns leading a group discussion about the situation you chose. Use the discussion-leading skills you learned (see Section 4B).

In each discussion:

- Talk about possible solutions for the situation (what the person *could* do).

- Decide which solution is best (what the person *should* do).

Step 3: Tell the class about the solution your group chose for each situation.

E   RESEARCH TOPICS

SLANG/JARGON* RESEARCH

Step 1: Choose a group of people who have their own slang (teenagers, college students) or jargon (computer programmers, medical professionals).

---

* *jargon:* technical words or phrases usually associated with a profession or field (e.g., computer jargon)

Step 2:   Interview a person from that group and take notes. Ask the person to tell you about special slang or jargon the group uses and to explain the meaning of five words or phrases. You can also find dictionaries of slang words on the Internet (keywords = *slang* and *jargon*) or in the library to add to your research.

Step 3:   Report to the class. Tell them what group of people you researched. Then write the slang or jargon on the board (but not the definitions). See if your classmates can guess the meaning of the words.

ACCENT INTERVIEW

Step 1:   Find a person who speaks with a different accent from the standard accent where you live. Interview the person about his or her accent. You can use the questions suggested below or some of your own.

1. Do you think you have an accent?

2. When did you first notice your accent?

3. What do people say about your accent?

4. Have you ever wanted to change your accent? Why or why not?

Step 2:   Discuss the results of your interview in small groups. How were the experiences of the people you interviewed similar to or different from Peter's experience? In what ways would the people you interviewed agree or disagree with Peter's opinions about accent and identity?

For Unit 5 Internet activities, visit the NorthStar Companion Website at http://www.longman.com/northstar.

Culture and Commerce

Long-necked women from the Pa Daung tribe wearing brass coils around their necks.

1 Focus on the Topic

A PREDICTING

Discuss these questions with the class.

1. What country are these women from?

2. The women are wearing coils around their necks. Why do you think they are wearing coils?

3. Read the title of this unit. What do you think the unit will be about?

B SHARING INFORMATION

1 *For each statement, give your opinion. Write **SD** (strongly disagree), **D** (disagree), **A** (agree), or **SA** (strongly agree) in each blank. Be prepared to give reasons to support your opinions.*

_____ **1.** Tourism can be harmful to the people living in a tourist area.

_____ **2.** People living in a tourist area can have better lives because of tourism.

_____ **3.** Tourist attractions* that harm people should not be allowed.

_____ **4.** Any tourist attraction that makes money should be allowed.

_____ **5.** Tourism is a good way for people to make money.

_____ **6.** Tourism destroys the natural environment.

2 *Discuss your answers for Exercise 1 in small groups. For which statements did you have different opinions?*

C PREPARING TO LISTEN

BACKGROUND

The little village of Nai Soi is home to the largest population of long-necked women in Northern Thailand. The village is near the border of Thailand and Myanmar (formerly Burma).

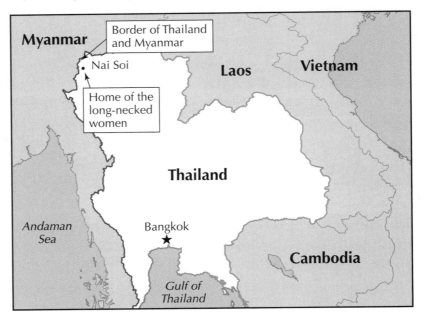

---

* **tourist attraction:** a special place or activity for tourists

1 *Read the following brochure for a tour to see the long-necked women.*

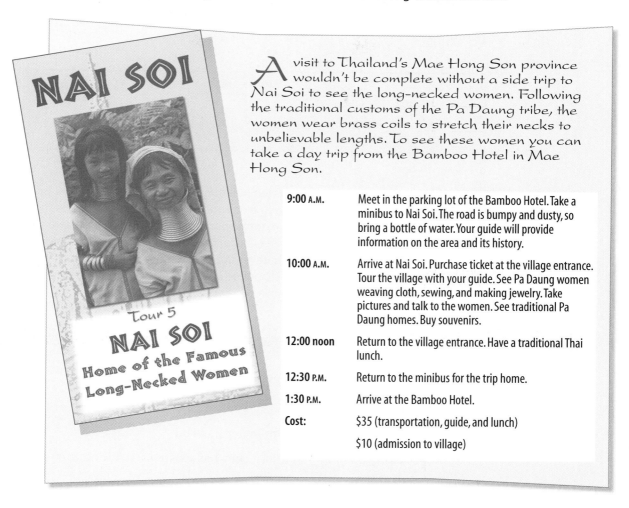

NAI SOI

Tour 5
NAI SOI
Home of the Famous
Long-Necked Women

A visit to Thailand's Mae Hong Son province wouldn't be complete without a side trip to Nai Soi to see the long-necked women. Following the traditional customs of the Pa Daung tribe, the women wear brass coils to stretch their necks to unbelievable lengths. To see these women you can take a day trip from the Bamboo Hotel in Mae Hong Son.

9:00 A.M.	Meet in the parking lot of the Bamboo Hotel. Take a minibus to Nai Soi. The road is bumpy and dusty, so bring a bottle of water. Your guide will provide information on the area and its history.
10:00 A.M.	Arrive at Nai Soi. Purchase ticket at the village entrance. Tour the village with your guide. See Pa Daung women weaving cloth, sewing, and making jewelry. Take pictures and talk to the women. See traditional Pa Daung homes. Buy souvenirs.
12:00 noon	Return to the village entrance. Have a traditional Thai lunch.
12:30 P.M.	Return to the minibus for the trip home.
1:30 P.M.	Arrive at the Bamboo Hotel.
Cost:	$35 (transportation, guide, and lunch)
	$10 (admission to village)

2 *Discuss these questions in small groups.*

1. Would you like to take this tour? Why or why not?

2. Does the price seem reasonable to you? Why or why not?

3. What are the positive aspects of this type of tourism? What are the negative aspects?

VOCABULARY FOR COMPREHENSION

Read the three e-mails that follow. Write the number of each underlined word next to its definition.

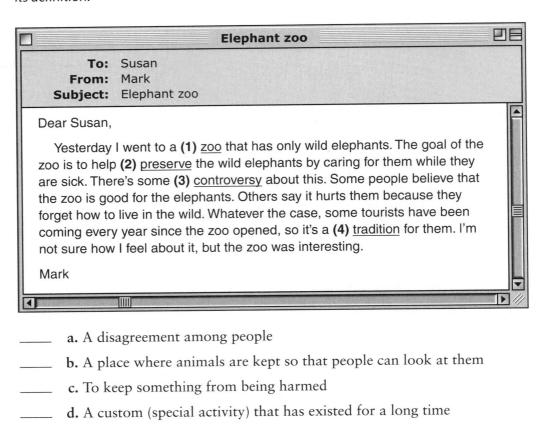

Elephant zoo

To: Susan
From: Mark
Subject: Elephant zoo

Dear Susan,

Yesterday I went to a **(1)** <u>zoo</u> that has only wild elephants. The goal of the zoo is to help **(2)** <u>preserve</u> the wild elephants by caring for them while they are sick. There's some **(3)** <u>controversy</u> about this. Some people believe that the zoo is good for the elephants. Others say it hurts them because they forget how to live in the wild. Whatever the case, some tourists have been coming every year since the zoo opened, so it's a **(4)** <u>tradition</u> for them. I'm not sure how I feel about it, but the zoo was interesting.

Mark

_____ **a.** A disagreement among people

_____ **b.** A place where animals are kept so that people can look at them

_____ **c.** To keep something from being harmed

_____ **d.** A custom (special activity) that has existed for a long time

Snake

To: Susan
From: Mark
Subject: Snake

Dear Susan,

This morning, I went to town to buy some **(5)** <u>souvenirs</u>. There was a man at the market with a large snake. The snake was **(6)** <u>wrapped</u> around his body about five times. I asked the man how long the snake was, so then he **(7)** <u>stretched</u> the snake out on the ground. It was more than eight feet long! I've never seen a snake that big before.

Mark

_____ **e.** Things you buy to help you remember a place

_____ **f.** Made longer by pulling

_____ **g.** Folded around something to cover it

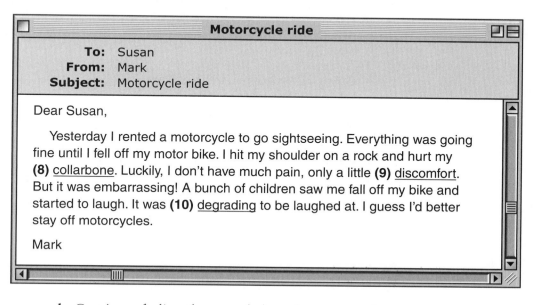

Motorcycle ride

To: Susan
From: Mark
Subject: Motorcycle ride

Dear Susan,

Yesterday I rented a motorcycle to go sightseeing. Everything was going fine until I fell off my motor bike. I hit my shoulder on a rock and hurt my **(8)** <u>collarbone</u>. Luckily, I don't have much pain, only a little **(9)** <u>discomfort</u>. But it was embarrassing! A bunch of children saw me fall off my bike and started to laugh. It was **(10)** <u>degrading</u> to be laughed at. I guess I'd better stay off motorcycles.

Mark

_____ **h.** Causing a feeling that people have lost respect for you

_____ **i.** A bone that goes from your neck to your shoulders

_____ **j.** A small pain

2 Focus on Listening

A LISTENING ONE: _Radio News Report_

 Listen to this excerpt from a news report. Circle your prediction.

This news report will present the tourist attraction in _____.
     a. a positive way
     b. a negative way
     c. a way that is both positive and negative

LISTENING FOR MAIN IDEAS

🎧 *Listen to the radio news report. Circle the best answer to complete each sentence.*

1. The long-necked women are important to northern Thailand because they _____.
   a. are good farmers
   b. bring money into the area
   c. work in restaurants

2. The Pa Daung women wear brass coils to _____.
   a. stretch their necks
   b. protect their necks
   c. hide their necks

3. If a long-necked woman takes off her brass coils, she will _____.
   a. be sent away from her village
   b. feel a lot of pain in her neck
   c. stop breathing

4. Some people feel that tourism helps the Pa Daung people to continue their traditions. Others say that tourism is _____.
   a. bad for the environment
   b. degrading to the Pa Daung women
   c. harmful to the Pa Daung men

LISTENING FOR DETAILS

🎧 *Listen to the radio report again. Write **T** (true) or **F** (false) for each statement. Compare your answers with a partner's.*

_____ 1. The Pa Daung people live in one small village on the border of Thailand and Myanmar.

_____ 2. About 100,000 tourists visit the long-necked women every year.

_____ 3. The long-necked women make money by selling souvenirs.

_____ 4. A full set of brass coils weighs 11 to 22 pounds (5 to 10 kilos).

_____ 5. A long-necked woman can take her neck coils off only to sleep.

_____ 6. The tradition of wrapping women's necks is still strong in Myanmar.

_____ 7. One long-necked woman said that she makes $70 to $80 a month.

_____ 8. Tourists at a hotel near Nai Soi had different opinions about whether or not to visit the long-necked women.

_____ 9. The reporter says that the Pa Daung will continue to wrap their daughters' necks as long as the tourists keep coming.

REACTING TO THE LISTENING

 1 *Listen to comments from two long-necked women. Focus on the tone of voice in each excerpt. How does each woman feel about her life? Describe the feelings by choosing adjectives from the list below. You may add your own adjectives if you wish. Explain your choices.*

| accepting | confused | frustrated | homesick | sad |
| angry | contented | happy | lucky | worried |

	ADJECTIVES TO DESCRIBE FEELINGS	EXPLANATION
Excerpt 1 Pa Peiy		
Excerpt 2 Ma Nang		

 2 *In the report, two tourists express different opinions about the long-necked women as a tourist attraction. Listen to their opinions and complete items 1–3 below.*

1. Write down each person's arguments.

SUPPORTS THE ATTRACTION (SANDRA)	OPPOSES THE ATTRACTION (FREDRICK)

2. Who do you agree with? Why?

3. Can you think of an additional argument to support your opinion? Write it down.

Discuss your answers with the class.

B LISTENING TWO: *Town Hall Meeting in Hyannis, Cape Cod*

Look at the information about Cape Cod. What can you conclude about this tourist destination?

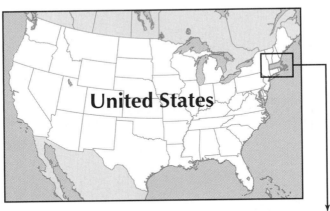

Cape Cod Region

Population: 210,000
Most important industry: Tourism
Number of tourists visiting Cape Cod each year: 5.3 million
Percentage of tourists coming between June and September: 65%
Percentage of jobs connected to tourism: 40%

Source: Center for Policy Analysis, University of Massachusetts, Dartmouth, MA, 2000.

Listening Two is an excerpt from a town hall meeting. The mayor (town leader) is leading the meeting. The townspeople are listening and expressing their opinions. Listen and circle the best answer to complete each sentence on page 99.

1. The first topic for discussion is _____.
   a. how to increase the number of tourists
   b. how to decrease the number of tourists
   c. the problems created by too many tourists

2. The traffic on Cape Cod _____.
   a. gets worse during the summer
   b. is bad all year
   c. is better now that there are buses

3. _____ is difficult to find on Cape Cod.
   a. Low-priced housing
   b. Housing for families
   c. Vacation housing

4. The woman who runs the souvenir shop does _____ percent of her business during the summer.
   a. 65
   b. 80
   c. 98

C LINKING LISTENINGS ONE AND TWO

Discuss the following questions in small groups. Discuss your answers with the class.

1. Listenings One and Two both present positive and negative aspects of tourism. What positive and negative aspects do they discuss? List the similarities in the chart below.

SIMILARITIES BETWEEN LISTENING ONE AND LISTENING TWO	
Positive Aspects of Tourism	**Negative Aspects of Tourism**

2. How would a decrease in tourism affect the long-necked women and the people of Cape Cod? In general, would a decline in tourism be good or bad for these people? What could they do if tourism declines?

3 Focus on Vocabulary

1 *A word can have a meaning that is positive (good), negative (bad), or neutral (neither good nor bad), for example:*

Positive	Negative	Neutral
beautiful	dirty	house

Now work in pairs. Complete the chart. Divide the words listed below into three groups: Positive, Negative, and Neutral.

attraction	discomfort	popular	tourism
controversy	farmer	preserve	tradition
degrading	harmful	souvenir	zoo

POSITIVE	NEGATIVE	NEUTRAL

2 *Compare your lists with those of another pair of students. Discuss the reasons for your choices.*

3 *Discuss the following questions in small groups. Make sure each person answers every question. Use the underlined words in your answer.*

1. What is the best or worst <u>souvenir</u> you have ever bought? Where did you buy it? Why did you buy it?

2. What is a <u>popular</u> <u>tourist</u> <u>attraction</u> in your country? Why is it popular?

3. Is there a <u>controversial</u> <u>tourist</u> <u>attraction</u> in your country? If so, what is it? Why is there a controversy about it?

4. How does <u>tourism</u> affect people in your country? Is it helpful, harmful, or not important to them? Why?

5. Sometimes <u>tourism</u> can help <u>preserve</u> <u>traditions</u>. What are some other ways to preserve traditions?

6. Can you think of an example of how <u>tourism</u> <u>harms</u> the environment? Can you think of an example of how it <u>preserves</u> the environment?

4 Focus on Speaking

A PRONUNCIATION: Past Tense Endings

The past tense ending -ed has three pronunciations.

Rules	Examples
1. Pronounce the **-ed** ending as /əd/ or /ɪd/ after verbs that end in /t/ or /d/.	**rented** (rent-əd) **folded** (fold-əd)
2. Pronounce the **-ed** ending as /t/ after verbs that end in voiceless consonants.	**worked** (work-t) **wrapped** (wrap-t)
3. Pronounce the **-ed** ending as /d/ after verbs that end in voiced consonants or in vowels.	**stayed** (stay-d) **lived** (live-d)
Note: Voiceless consonants are /p, t, k, f, s, θ, ʃ, h, tʃ/. Voiced consonants are /b, d, g, ð, v, z, ʒ, dʒ, n, m, ŋ, r, l, w, y/.	

1 *Listen and repeat the past tense verbs. Then write each verb in the correct column in the chart below.*

1. harmed	4. invited	7. visited	10. wrapped
2. allowed	5. improved	8. stretched	11. talked
3. helped	6. ended	9. rubbed	12. attracted

/əd/	/t/	/d/
		harmed

2 *Check your answers with a partner. Take turns reading the verbs in each column out loud.*

3 *Listen to and repeat the sentences. Write the verb you hear in the blank. Take turns reading the sentences to a partner.*

1. We met a long-necked woman who _____ about her experience.

2. She said that when she was five years old, her mother _____ a brass coil around her neck.

3. The coil _____ out her neck.

4. It was uncomfortable, but it _____ a lot of tourists.

5. The money from the tourists _____ her life.

6. The woman _____ us to take photos.

7. She _____ us to visit her house.

8. Our visit _____ after we bought some souvenirs.

B   STYLE: Transitions for Storytelling

Transition words are used to tell the listener when a new event is about to happen in a story. They are usually placed at the beginning of a sentence.

Example: Ma Nang, a long-necked woman, remembers the day she received her first brass coils. "I was 5 years old," she says. "The day *began when* I had a special meal. *Then* my mother and my aunt put oil on my neck and rubbed it. *When* my muscles were loose, they pulled my head to stretch my neck. *After* several hours of rubbing and pulling, they took me outside where the whole village was waiting. *Then* the brass coils were wrapped around my neck. *When* the day *ended*, I was a long-necked girl.

Certain transition words are used to tell about events that happen at the beginning of a story, others tell about events at the end, and others show the events that happen in between. Use the following words to show when events occur in a story.

Beginning	In between	Ending
First, . . .	After . . .	Finally, . . .
. . . began when . . .	After that, . . .	In / At the end, . . .
To begin with . . .	Then . . .	. . . ended when . . .
	Next, . . .	At last . . .
	When . . .	

Sit in a circle in groups of three or four. Take turns reading a section of the story below. Add transition words in each blank space. Think of details to add to the story.

Example: This was my first day in Thailand. <u>My day began when</u> I arrived in

Bangkok at 10:00 A.M. My trip was <u>very long and I was tired.</u>

1. _____ I took a taxi to my hotel. The hotel was . . .

2. _____ I took a nap. I slept . . .

3. _____ I went to the market to buy souvenirs. I bought . . .

4. _____ I ate dinner. The restaurant was . . .

5. _____ I walked around the city. I saw . . .

6. _____ I got lost going back to the hotel, I asked . . .

7. _____ I found my hotel. I went . . .

C   GRAMMAR: Simple Past Tense

1 *Read the e-mail about Susan's most recent vacation. Circle the past tense verbs. Then answer the questions.*

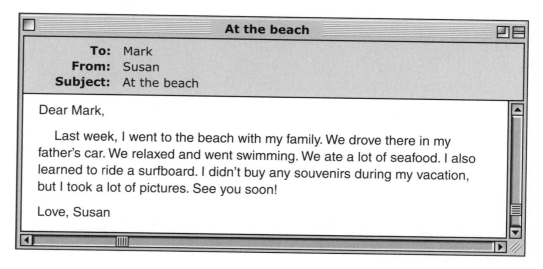

1. How many past tense verbs did you circle?

2. Some of the verbs end with *-ed* and some do not. What is the difference between these two types of verbs?

Simple Past Tense	Examples
1. Use the simple past tense to talk about actions, states, and situations in the past that are now finished.	Last week, Susan **went** to the beach.
2. To form the simple past with regular verbs, add **-d** or **-ed** to the base form of the verb.	She **relaxed**. She **learned** to ride a surfboard.
3. To form the simple past with irregular verbs, use the irregular past tense form.	She **took** a lot of pictures. Other irregular verbs: have → had make → made go → went eat → ate
4. To form a negative, add **did not** or **didn't** before the base form of the verb.	She **didn't buy** any souvenirs.

2 *Work with a partner. Take turns interviewing each other about your most recent vacations. Use past tense verbs.*

1. When did you go on your most recent vacation?
2. Where did you go?
3. How did you get there?
4. Who went with you?
5. What did you do?
6. What kind of souvenirs did you buy?
7. What did you like and dislike about the vacation?

3 *Share information about your partner's vacation with the class. Which students did the following things? Give examples.*

1. Who spent the longest amount of time on vacation?
2. Who traveled the longest distance during the vacation?
3. Who had the most unusual vacation?

4. Who had the most relaxing vacation?

5. Who had the most problems during the vacation?

6. Who was most active (doing sports and other physical activities) during the vacation?

7. Who went on vacation with the largest group of people?

8. Who bought the most souvenirs on vacation?

9. Other: _____ ?

D SPEAKING TOPIC

Give a two- to three-minute oral presentation to tell the class about a tourist experience you have had.

CHOOSING A TOPIC

Introduce your presentation with the sentence that follows. Use an adjective from the box or one of your own.

embarrassing	exciting	humorous
enjoyable	frightening	memorable
exhausting	frustrating	unusual

The most _____ tourist experience I've ever had was when I went
            (adjective)

to _____.
   (place)

PREPARING

Prepare your presentation using the outline on page 106.

Step 1: Introduction—Introduce your topic with the sentence you completed above. Then give other information to support your topic (when you traveled, who you traveled with, and so on).

Step 2: Body—Write the events of your experience in order. Include the transitions you will use (see Section 4B).

Step 3: Conclusion—Restate the topic in a summary sentence. Then, in a concluding sentence, explain what you learned from your experience or whether you would do it again.

Outline

Introduction

1. Topic: "The most _____ tourist experience I've ever had was

when I went to _____."

2. Other information: _____

_____

_____

Body

Events:

_____.

_____.

_____.

_____.

_____.

_____.

_____.

_____.

Conclusion

1. Summary sentence: "So that was the most _____ tourist

experience I've ever had."

2. Concluding sentence: _____

_____

_____

PRACTICING

Step 1: Practice telling your story out loud. Use your outline to help remind you of your ideas. Remember to use the past tense (see Sections 4A and 4C) and transitions between events (see Section 4B).

Step 2: Keep practicing until you feel comfortable and do not need to use your notes very much. Make sure your presentation is about two minutes long. Add or take away parts of the story to stay within the time frame.

PRESENTING

Give your oral presentation to the class.

Listening Task

As you listen to other students' presentations, write down a question to ask each presenter when he or she finishes.

E RESEARCH TOPICS

POSTER PRESENTATION

Step 1: Choose a tourist attraction in or near the place where you live. Visit tourist information centers and travel agencies to collect brochures and information about your attraction.

Step 2: Use the brochures to prepare a poster. Include the following information:

- The name of the attraction

- What you can do there

- Any other interesting information (historical information, best times to visit, and so on)

- The positive and negative effects of the tourist attraction on people or the environment

Step 3: Hang your posters on the classroom wall. Half the students will stand next to their posters and present their information. The other students will walk around and learn about different tourist attractions. Switch roles after 15 or 20 minutes.

SURVEY

Step 1: Choose a popular tourist attraction in or near the place where you live. Find three people who are familiar with the attraction. If possible, find someone who works with tourists there.

Step 2: Ask each person these questions. Tape-record the answers.

- Why is this place so popular with tourists?

- What are some of the positive effects of tourism in this area?

- What are some of the negative effects of tourism in this area?

- In general, is this tourist destination good or bad for the community?

Step 3: Prepare a short presentation of your survey results for the class.

For Unit 6 Internet activities, visit the NorthStar Companion Website at http://www.longman.com/northstar.

Joking Around

1 Focus on the Topic

A PREDICTING

Look at the cartoon and discuss these questions with the class.

1. A joke is something funny that you say to make people laugh. How would you explain the joke in the cartoon?

2. Do you think the cartoon is funny? Why or why not?

3. Read the title of this unit. What do you think the unit will be about?

B   SHARING INFORMATION

Discuss with a partner or in small groups.

1. Humor is something that is funny. A joke is one kind of humor. Check (✓) the types of humor you like, and add others.

    _____ **a.** television or movie comedies

    _____ **b.** cartoons on TV or in a magazine or newspaper

    _____ **c.** comic strips in the newspaper

    _____ **d.** jokes

    _____ **e.** stand-up comedy in front of an audience

    _____ **f.** other _____

2. What kinds of humor do you dislike? Why?

3. What kinds of humor are popular in your culture?

C   PREPARING TO LISTEN

BACKGROUND

Look at these different types of jokes. Pay attention to the punch line, which is the funny statement at the end of a joke.

Pun

A **pun** is a joke that uses a word with two meanings in the punch line.

Riddle

A **riddle** is a puzzle with a funny answer.

Knock-Knock Joke

A **knock-knock joke** begins with "knock knock" and ends with a pun.

Light Bulb Joke

A **light bulb joke** begins with the question "How many _____ does it take to change a light bulb?" This kind of joke usually makes fun of certain professions or groups of people.

HOW MANY FIREFIGHTERS DOES IT TAKE TO CHANGE A LIGHTBULB?

FOUR. ONE TO CHANGE THE BULB AND THREE TO CUT A HOLE IN THE ROOF.

Discuss these questions with the class.

1. Look at the pun cartoon. What is the punch line in this cartoon? Which word has two meanings? What are they?

2. Look at the riddle cartoon. Is this riddle funny? Can you explain why?

3. Look at the knock-knock joke cartoon. How does the person answer "knock-knock"? What is the pun?

4. Look at the light bulb joke cartoon. What group or profession is talked about in this joke? What does this joke say about the group or profession?

VOCABULARY FOR COMPREHENSION

Read the conversations. Then circle the best answer to complete each definition of the underlined words.

1. A: Humorous TV shows are really popular.
   B: I guess our <u>society</u> likes to laugh.

   A <u>society</u> is a _____.
   a. group of people   **b.** good friend

2. A: My son is having problems in school.
   B: You'd better <u>deal with</u> it now or it will become a bigger problem later.

   To <u>deal with</u> something means to _____.
   a. ignore a problem   **b.** take action to solve a problem

3. A: I went to a great party last night. I talked to so many people.
   B: I'm glad I didn't go. I don't like to <u>socialize</u>; I prefer to stay home.

   To <u>socialize</u> means to spend time _____.
      a. alone   **b.** with other people

4. A: Those two children really <u>bonded</u> with each other.
   B: Yes. They have become very good friends.

   To <u>bond</u> means to _____ with someone.
      a. develop a special   **b.** spend a lot of time
          relationship

5. A: Why did the chicken cross the road?
   B: I <u>give up</u>.
   A: To get to the other side!

   To <u>give up</u> means to _____.
      a. have an opinion   **b.** not know the answer

6. A: That bowl looks old.
   B: Yes. It's <u>ancient</u>. It's more than 800 years old!

   If something is <u>ancient</u>, it is _____.
      a. very old   **b.** easy to break

7. A: I've just discovered a new <u>category</u> of jokes. They're called knock-knock jokes.
   B: Oh, yeah! Those are the jokes that all begin with "Knock knock."

   A <u>category</u> is _____.
      a. something or someone   **b.** a group of people or
          that everyone knows   things that are similar

8. A: Those girls were laughing at my accent.
   B: Sounds like they were <u>making fun of</u> you. Just ignore them.

   To <u>make fun of</u> someone means to _____.
      a. make the person laugh   **b.** laugh at the person

9. A: I don't like religious jokes. They're <u>offensive</u>.
   B: I think they're funny. But if I were religious, I wouldn't like them, either.

   If something is <u>offensive</u>, it is _____.
      a. very rude and likely to   **b.** hard to understand
          upset someone

10. A: My daughter always has to wear the same kinds of clothes as her friends.
    B: Don't worry. It's just her way of showing <u>solidarity</u>.

    To show <u>solidarity</u> means to _____.
       a. show support for a group   **b.** show that you are strong
           that you belong to

2 Focus on Listening

A LISTENING ONE: *What's So Funny?*

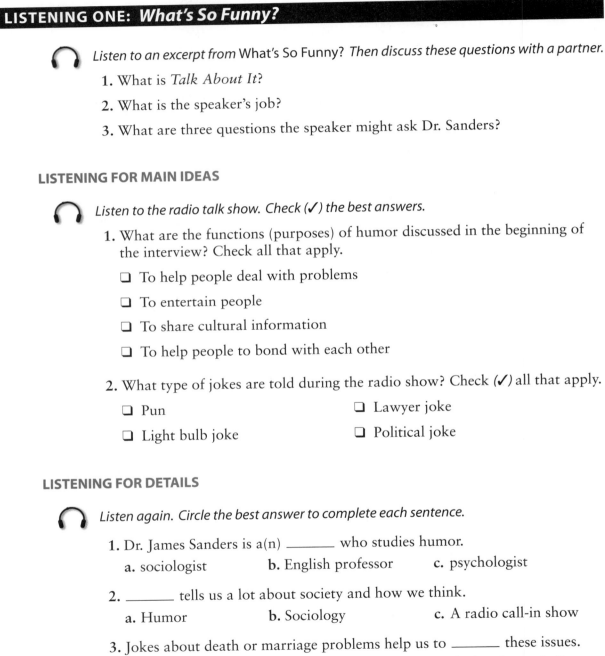

Listen to an excerpt from What's So Funny? *Then discuss these questions with a partner.*

1. What is *Talk About It*?

2. What is the speaker's job?

3. What are three questions the speaker might ask Dr. Sanders?

LISTENING FOR MAIN IDEAS

Listen to the radio talk show. Check (✓) the best answers.

1. What are the functions (purposes) of humor discussed in the beginning of the interview? Check all that apply.

❏ To help people deal with problems

❏ To entertain people

❏ To share cultural information

❏ To help people to bond with each other

2. What type of jokes are told during the radio show? Check (✓) all that apply.

❏ Pun   ❏ Lawyer joke

❏ Light bulb joke   ❏ Political joke

LISTENING FOR DETAILS

Listen again. Circle the best answer to complete each sentence.

1. Dr. James Sanders is a(n) _____ who studies humor.
    a. sociologist   **b.** English professor   **c.** psychologist

2. _____ tells us a lot about society and how we think.
    a. Humor   **b.** Sociology   **c.** A radio call-in show

3. Jokes about death or marriage problems help us to _____ these issues.
    a. forget about   **b.** remember   **c.** deal with our feelings about

4. People enjoy the _____ of laughter.
    a. sound   **b.** feeling   **c.** results

5. Andrew is _____ years old.
   a. seven   **b.** nine   **c.** eleven

6. Puns are a(n) _____ type of humor.
   a. ancient   **b.** offensive   **c.** simple

7. Joan is a _____.
   a. lawyer   **b.** teacher   **c.** firefighter

8. Joan tells a joke that has _____ questions.
   a. two   **b.** three   **c.** four

9. Jokes about a group of people usually make fun of _____.
   a. rich people   **b.** the group   **c.** one person

10. Sometimes it's OK to tell a joke about a group of people if _____.
    a. you belong to that group   **b.** the group is big   **c.** the joke is really funny

REACTING TO THE LISTENING

Irony is saying the opposite of what you really mean in order to be funny. A speaker shows irony by using tone of voice.

 1 Listen to the excerpts. Check (✔) whether the second speaker in each excerpt is being ironic or serious. Then explain how the speaker's tone of voice helped you understand his or her feelings.

	IRONIC	SERIOUS	TONE OF VOICE
Excerpt 1 Dr. Sanders (sociologist)	❑	❑	
Excerpt 2 Dr. Sanders (sociologist)	❑	❑	
Excerpt 3 Joan (caller)	❑	❑	
Excerpt 4 Carmen (radio host)	❑	❑	

2 *Discuss in small groups. Do you agree with Dr. Sanders' opinions in the following quotes? Why or why not? Share your opinions with the class.*

1. "Well, we often make jokes about things we're uncomfortable with. . . . They help us deal with our feelings about these issues."

2. " . . . mostly, humor is a way for people to socialize. . . . It's a way for people to connect—a way to bond with each other."

3. "People often make jokes about their own group as a way of showing group solidarity. . . ."

B   LISTENING TWO: *More Jokes*

 Listen to more jokes. Match each joke with its punch line. Check your answers with the class.

Joke

_____ Joke 1

_____ Joke 2

_____ Joke 3

_____ Joke 4

_____ Joke 5

_____ Joke 6

_____ Joke 7

_____ Joke 8

Punch Line

a. All the information you need—but you can't understand a word of it.

b. Six. One to change the bulb and five to ask for directions.

c. A zebra rolling down a hill with a leaf in its mouth.

d. Impossible!

e. Avenue heard this joke before?

f. An elephant's shadow.

g. Forty-five. One to change the bulb and 44 to do the paperwork.

h. You're welcome!

C   LINKING LISTENINGS ONE AND TWO

1 *In Section 1C and in Listening One, there are descriptions of different types of jokes. Listen again to Listening Two. Match the punch line with the type of joke. Then discuss your answers with the class.*

Joke

_____ Joke 1

_____ Joke 2

_____ Joke 3

_____ Joke 4

_____ Joke 5

_____ Joke 6

_____ Joke 7

_____ Joke 8

Type of Joke

a. Knock-knock

b. Riddle

c. Light bulb

d. Lawyer

2 *Think of the jokes you heard in Listenings One and Two. Which one do you think was the funniest? Why?*

3 Focus on Vocabulary

1 *Complete the sentences with words from the box below. Fill in the missing words in the crossword puzzle.*

ancient	comedy	humor	punch line
bond	comic	ironic	riddle
cartoon	deal with	make fun	socialize
category	give up	offensive	solidarity

Across

2. I don't like jokes about ethnic groups. I think they are _____.

3. I tried to tell a joke, but I couldn't. I forgot the _____.

5. My favorite _____ of jokes is riddles.

7. I like to go to parties and _____ with my friends.

8. Kids at school used to _____ of me. They called me "stupid" and other mean names.

9. Here's a _____: "What goes around the house but never moves?"

11. Sometimes people tell jokes about their group to show _____ between the members.

15. It's good to keep a sense of _____ and not be serious all the time.

16. I _____. I don't know the answer to this riddle.

Down

1. I like to watch _____ shows on TV.

4. Mickey Mouse is my favorite _____ character.

6. When I am sad, I _____ my feelings by watching a funny movie.

10. I like to read the _____ strips in the morning paper.

12. He didn't mean what he said. He was being _____.

13. Puns are a very _____ type of joke. They have existed for many years.

14. When I'm in a new class, one way we _____ together is by making jokes about our teacher.

2 *Think of at least one example for each situation below. Share your examples in small groups. Give yourself one point for each example you think of. The person with the most points at the end wins.*

Think of an example of a/an:

1. Ancient joke or pun

2. Category of joke not mentioned in Section 1C

3. Time someone used humor to show solidarity or closeness with a group of people

4. Ironic statement

5. Subject studied by a sociologist

6. Person famous for his or her sense of humor

7. Comedy show on TV

8. Cartoon you enjoyed as a child

9. Comic strip you can read in the newspaper

10. Joke with a funny punch line

11. Place or situation in which humor should not be used

12. Animal riddle

4 Focus on Speaking

A   PRONUNCIATION: Reduction of *h* in Pronouns

Pronouns are usually unstressed when we speak.

Pronouns beginning with the letter *h*—*he, him, her, his*—usually lose the /h/ sound when they are inside a sentence. They are then connected to the ending of the preceding word.

Examples: What's h̸is name? ("Whatsis name?")

What did h̸e do? ("What diddy do?")

1 *Listen and repeat.*

1. Where did h̸e go? (say "Where diddy go?")

2. What's h̸er name? (say "Whatser name?")

3. I heard h̸is jokes. (say "I herdis jokes.")

4. They made fun of h̸im. (say "They made fun ovim.")

5. He told h̸er a riddle. (say "He tolder a riddle.")

2 *Listen to the following knock-knock jokes. Notice that the pronouns in the punch lines are connected to preceding words. Repeat each line. In the blank provided, rewrite the punch line for each joke, using the correct pronoun.*

1. Knock knock.
   Who's there?
   Izzy.
   Izzy who?
   Izzy home?
   _Is he home?_____

2. Knock knock.
   Who's there?
   Teller.
   Teller who?
   Teller I'm here.
   _____

3. Knock knock.
   Who's there?
   Callim.
   Callim who?
   Callim today.
   _____

4. Knock knock.
   Who's there?
   Writer.
   Writer who?
   Writer a letter.
   _____

5. Knock knock.
   Who's there?
   Tellis.
   Tellis who?
   Tellis mother to come.

———————————————

3 *Check your punch lines from Exercise 2 with a partner. Then take turns telling the jokes.*

4 *Write three knock-knock jokes. You may use the prompts below or make up your own.*

Duzzy (does he)
Givis (give his)
Getim (get him)
Lender (lend her)

Diddy (did he)
Leevim (leave him)
Sender (send her)
Askis (ask his)

Walk around the room. Tell your jokes to three classmates.

B   STYLE: Asking for Repetition or Clarification

If you don't hear or don't understand what someone is saying, you can ask the person to repeat. If you want someone to explain, or clarify, something, you can ask for clarification. Use these questions to ask for repetition and clarification.

Asking for Repetition	Asking for Clarification
Excuse me?	I'm sorry, what do you mean by _____?
I'm sorry, what did you say?	I'm sorry, what does _____ mean?
Would you repeat that, please?	I'm sorry, I don't understand what you mean by _____.
Sorry?	

1 *Fill in the blanks with your own information.*

1. I _____ (*like/don't like*) watching comedies because _____

_____ .

2. My top three favorite movies are _____

_____ .

3. I like _____ jokes because _____

_____ .

4. I don't like _____ jokes because _____

_____ .

5. In my country it's not OK to tell jokes about _____

because _____ .

2 *Work in pairs. Sit with your back to your partner.*

Student A

Read your sentences from Exercise 1 quickly. Stop after each sentence so that your partner can ask for repetition or clarification.

Student B

Listen to your partner's sentences and fill in the information below. If you don't hear or understand what your partner says, ask for repetition and/or clarification.

1. My partner _____ (*likes/doesn't like*) watching comedies

because _____ .

2. My partner's top three favorite movies are _____

_____ .

3. My partner likes _____ jokes because _____

_____ .

4. My partner doesn't like _____ jokes because _____

_____ .

5. In my partner's country it's not OK to tell jokes about _____

because _____ .

Change roles and repeat the activity. Then compare notes to see if you heard and understood each other correctly.

C GRAMMAR: *Wh-* Questions

1 *Discuss these questions with the class.*

1. Who is the man in the photograph?

2. Where does he live?

3. What does he do?

2 *Look again at the questions from Exercise 1. Use them to answer the questions below.*

1. Circle the first word of each question. How are these words similar?

2. These are *wh-* questions. What is another name for *wh-* questions?

Wh- Questions	Examples
Use **wh-** questions to ask for specific information.	Some **wh-** question words are *who(m), what, where, when, which, why,* and *how.*
When you ask about the subject: Use a **wh-** question word in place of the subject.	**Jerry Seinfeld** lives in New York. **Who** lives in New York?
When you ask about the predicate: Use *yes/no* question order, but begin with a **wh-** word.	Jerry Seinfeld lives **in New York.** Does Jerry Seinfeld live in New York? **Where** does Jerry Seinfeld live?

3 *Work in pairs. Student A reads the directions below. Student B uses the instructions in Student Activities on page 183.*

*Student A: Read the biography of comedian Jerry Seinfeld. Then write **wh-** questions to find out the missing information from your partner. Ask your partner the questions and fill in the information. Then answer your partner's questions.*

Jerry Seinfeld was born on (**1**) _____, in the city of New York. He grew up in Brooklyn, and after high school he studied at (**2**) _____.

One of Jerry's earliest jobs was to call people over the phone to sell them light bulbs. When people sent in money, (**3**) _____ kept it but didn't send any bulbs. In another job, Jerry sold cheap jewelry on the street and pretended that it was expensive.

This dark period in Jerry's life did not last long. He began telling jokes at a comedy club called "Catch a Rising Star," which is how he became a star himself. Later, he was invited to perform on two famous late-night talk shows because (**4**) _____. And before long he had his own TV show, called *Seinfeld*. The show was so successful that it won an Emmy award in 1993 for Best Comedy Show. Since then he has won many other awards.

Jerry does not smoke or drink. He is married to (**5**) _____, who works as a public relations executive. They have a daughter named Sascha. Today, (**6**) _____ feels that life is just about perfect!

Questions

1. *When was Jerry Seinfeld born?* _____

2. _____

3. _____

4. _____

5. _____

6. _____

D SPEAKING TOPIC

Work in ten small groups. You will tell a joke to your classmates.

Step 1: Each group will be assigned a number from 1 to 10. Find the jokes for your group in Student Activities on pages 184–185. Choose the one your group likes best. (Don't read the other groups' jokes.)

Step 2: Walk around the room. Find someone from another group. Take turns telling the jokes that your groups chose. Leave out the punch lines. Listen to your partner's joke and try to guess the punch line. You may ask your partner to repeat the joke (see Section 4B). If you can't guess the punch line, say, "I give up," and have your partner tell you the punch line.

Step 3: After you hear the punch line, respond to the joke by saying, "I don't get it," "That's funny," or "That's very funny." Then check (✓) the corresponding box in the chart below.

Step 4: Continue until you have heard jokes from all the groups.

GROUP NUMBER	I DON'T GET IT.	THAT'S FUNNY.	THAT'S VERY FUNNY.
1			
2			
3			
4			
5			
6			
7			
8			
9			
10			

Step 5: As a class, discuss the meaning of each joke. Vote on the funniest.

E RESEARCH TOPICS

JOKE SEARCH

Search for jokes on the Internet. Here are some suggested key words for your search: *humor, jokes, riddles, puns.* Choose a joke that you like. Print it or write it down. Bring the joke to class and tell it to your classmates.

JOKE TRANSLATION

Think of a joke from your culture that translates into English (puns probably won't work). Write the joke down and bring it to class. Tell the joke and post it on the wall so that other students can learn it.

For Unit 7 Internet activities, visit the NorthStar Companion Website at http://www.longman.com/northstar.

Traditional or Trendy?

1 Focus on the Topic

A PREDICTING

Look at the photographs and discuss these questions with the class.

1. Where might this woman wear her different outfits?

2. What do *traditional* and *trendy* mean?

3. What do you think this unit will be about?

B   SHARING INFORMATION

Discuss these questions in small groups.

1. In your culture, what would you wear in the following places?

   - an expensive restaurant
   - a wedding
   - your home
   - a grocery store
   - a school

2. In your culture do women or men ever wear traditional clothing? What does it look like? When do they wear it?

C   PREPARING TO LISTEN

BACKGROUND

Sri Lanka is a small island off the coast of India. It has about 20 million people. The capital city is Colombo. The country's two main ethnic* groups are the Sinhalese (about 74% of the population) and the Tamils (about 18% of the population).

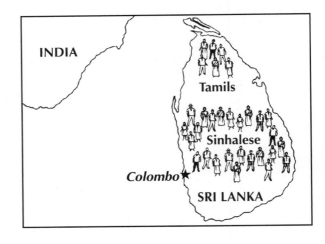

The traditional clothing for a Sri Lankan woman is a sari. It is a long piece of silky cloth that is wrapped around the body. For men, the traditional clothing is a sarong. It is shorter than a sari. It is usually made of cotton cloth and is wrapped around the waist.

Discuss these questions with the class.

1. Is the traditional clothing in Sri Lanka similar to the traditional clothing of other countries? If so, which countries?

2. In Sri Lanka and many other countries, more and more people are wearing Western clothing instead of traditional clothing. What are the advantages and disadvantages of traditional clothing?

Sari

Sarong

---

ethnic: relating to a particular race or culture

VOCABULARY FOR COMPREHENSION

Match each underlined word with a definition or synonym listed below. Write the correct letter in the blank.

a. to affect the way someone behaves or thinks

b. opinions and feelings you have about something

c. being the only one of its kind

d. important events

e. unusual or exciting because of a connection with a foreign country

f. the importance or usefulness of something

g. sensible and useful

h. to be likely to do something

i. to spend time with

j. modern and fashionable

—— 1. I <u>tend to</u> wear dresses in the summer. In fact, I hardly ever wear pants.

—— 2. Traditional clothing isn't <u>practical</u> to wear for exercising because it's difficult to move around in.

—— 3. He likes to wear traditional clothes for special <u>occasions</u> like holidays and religious celebrations.

—— 4. When I <u>hang out</u> with my friends, we usually like to go to the movies or go out to eat.

—— 5. Everyone is wearing jeans these days, so that's what I wear. I guess you can say that my friends <u>influence</u> what I wear.

—— 6. People's <u>attitudes</u> toward traditional clothing can change. Sometimes they want to wear it, and sometimes they don't.

—— 7. When I was a child, I didn't understand the <u>value</u> of traditional clothes. I thought they were useless.

—— 8. Teenagers like to be <u>in style</u>. They usually try to wear the latest fashions.

—— 9. This dress is <u>unique</u>. No one else has a dress like it.

—— 10. I like to wear my traditional clothing in the United States because people think it's <u>exotic</u>. Sometimes it's fun to wear something from a different culture.

2 Focus on Listening

A   LISTENING ONE: *Interview with Shanika De Silva*

 You will hear an interview with Shanika De Silva about traditional clothes in Sri Lanka. Listen to this excerpt from the interview and discuss the following questions with a partner.

1. Where is Shanika living?

2. What do you think Shanika might say about traditional dress? Make a prediction.

LISTENING FOR MAIN IDEAS

 Below is a list of things that could influence people to wear or not wear traditional clothing. Listen to the interview and check (✓) six topics that Shanika mentions. Compare your answers with a partner's.

_____ 1. age

_____ 2. comfort/discomfort

_____ 3. pressure from family

_____ 4. desire to be modern

_____ 5. cost

_____ 6. friends

_____ 7. family background

_____ 8. city life/country life

_____ 9. opinion of husband or wife

_____ 10. desire to connect with your culture

LISTENING FOR DETAILS

 *Listen again. Decide if each statement is true or false. Write **T** (true) or **F** (false). Compare your answers with a partner's.*

_____ 1. Shanika lives in the United States now.

_____ 2. A sari goes around your waist and over one shoulder.

_____ 3. Saris are cool and easy to move around in.

_____ 4. Older women tend to wear saris.

___ 5. Many younger women in Sri Lanka want to be modern.

___ 6. Sinhalese and Tamil women tend to wear Western clothing.

___ 7. A sarong often has a zipper in the back.

___ 8. Today most men wear sarongs to their jobs in the city.

___ 9. Shanika wore a sari for her wedding.

___ 10. When she was younger, Shanika didn't like to wear saris.

REACTING TO THE LISTENING

 1 *According to Shanika, people from Sri Lanka have both positive and negative feelings about traditional clothing. Listen to the following excerpts from the interview. For each excerpt, circle the number that best describes Shanika's feelings (**1** = positive, **2** = not positive, not negative, **3** = negative). As you listen, write down words and phrases that influence your answers. Listen also to Shanika's tone of voice for information about her feelings.*

	POSITIVE		NEGATIVE	WORDS, PHRASES, AND TONE OF VOICE
Excerpt 1	1	2	3	
Excerpt 2	1	2	3	
Excerpt 3	1	2	3	
Excerpt 4	1	2	3	

Compare your answers as a class. Did everyone agree? Why or why not?

2 *Work in small groups. Read the quotations from the listening and discuss the questions.*

1. "People who live in the countryside still wear sarongs. But in the city, men wear pants and shirts."

    a. Is the same thing happening in your culture? Is Western clothing replacing traditional clothing?

    b. Should people be encouraged to wear traditional clothing rather than Western dress? Why or why not?

2. "When you're older, you can see the value in traditional clothing more. When you're younger, you're more interested in being in style."

    a. Do you agree with the statement?

    b. Do you like to wear traditional clothing from your culture? Why or why not?

B LISTENING TWO: *Interview with a Fashion Designer*

1 *Look at the illustrations. The words that are underlined appear in the listening. Guess the meaning of these words and discuss your ideas with the class.*

Polo shirts have a **casual** look.

Sweaters are comfortable yet **stylish**.

2 *In Listening Two, a reporter talks to a fashion designer. Listen and circle the correct answers to complete each sentence.*

1. The reporter and the fashion designer are _____.

    a. at the designer's office

    b. at a radio studio

    c. at a fashion show

2. The interview is about men's casual clothing for _____.
   a. wearing at home
   b. the workplace
   c. parties

3. About _____ of big companies are allowing employees to wear casual clothes.
   a. 25%
   b. 50%
   c. 75%

4. Casual office clothing needs to be _____.
   a. comfortable and stylish
   b. colorful and bright
   c. traditional and serious

5. Employees in casual offices tend to work _____ hours.
   a. longer
   b. shorter
   c. the same number of

6. _____ of the supervisors wear casual clothes.
   a. Almost all
   b. None
   c. Some

C   LINKING LISTENINGS ONE AND TWO

How would Shanika De Silva and Marco Bellini respond to the statements below? Answer the questions and discuss your thoughts with the class.

STATEMENT	SHANIKA'S OPINION	MARCO'S OPINION
"Traditional clothing is not useful in a modern world."	*Would Shanika agree? Why or why not?*	*Would Marco agree? Why or why not?*
"There has been a worldwide trend (change) toward wearing more casual clothing."	*According to Shanika, what is the reason for this trend in Sri Lanka?*	*According to Marco, what is the reason for this trend in the workplace?*

3 Focus on Vocabulary

An analogy shows relationships between words. Below are four types of analogies that show different kinds of relationships.

Types of Analogies

1. **Action/Object.** Shows what action is used with an object.

   fly : plane :: drive : car
   Fly is to *plane* as *drive* is to *car*.

   You **fly** a **plane**. You **drive** a **car**.

2. **Opposite.** Shows two opposite things.

   love : hate :: fast : slow
   Love is to *hate* as *fast* is to *slow*.

   The opposite of **love** is **hate**. The opposite of **fast** is **slow**.

3. **Description.** Shows what something is by describing it.

   water : wet :: ice : cold
   Water is to *wet* as *ice* is to *cold*.

   Water is **wet**. **Ice** is **cold**.

4. **Part/Whole.** Shows a small part of something larger.

   student : class :: eye : body
   Student is to *class* as *eye* is to *body*.

   A **student** is part of a **class**. An **eye** is part of the **body**.

1 *Work with a partner. Choose the correct word from the box below to complete each analogy on page 135. For each analogy, write two explanation sentences like those above.*

casual	handbag	modern	sarong
comfortable	influence	old-fashioned	Sri Lanka
designer	jeans	sari	value

Example: London : United Kingdom :: Colombo : _____*Sri Lanka*_____

Explanation sentences: _*London is the capital of the United Kingdom.*_
*Colombo is the capital of Sri Lanka.*

1. practical : impractical :: modern : _____

   Explanation sentences: _____

   _____

2. put on : pants :: wrap : _____

   Explanation sentences: _____

   _____

3. man : sarong :: woman : _____

   Explanation sentences: _____

   _____

4. sari : traditional :: jeans : _____

   Explanation sentences: _____

   _____

5. Coke : soft drink :: Levi's : _____

   Explanation sentences: _____

   _____

6. strong : weak :: formal : _____

   Explanation sentences: _____

   _____

7. wear : sarong :: carry : _____

   Explanation sentences: _____

   _____

8. high heels : uncomfortable :: athletic shoes : _____

   Explanation sentences: _____

   _____

2 *Work in small groups. Read the nouns and adjectives in the list. Discuss the meanings of any words you don't know. (Use a dictionary if necessary.) Write each word on a separate slip of paper. Fold up the slips and put them in a container. Then cover the list so you can't see it.*

Nouns		Adjectives	
athletic shoes	(a) model	casual	practical
designer	pants	exotic	stylish
handbag	sarong	formal	traditional
high heels	shorts	modern	trendy
jeans	shoulder	offbeat	unique
miniskirt	T-shirt	old-fashioned	Western

One student draws a slip from the container and tells the part of speech (noun or adjective). The student gives clues about the word.

- Clues can only be single words or short phrases.
- You cannot say any of the words on the paper.

After each clue, the rest of the group discusses together and then guesses the word. The goal is to guess the word with as few clues as possible. Take turns picking papers and giving clues.

Example: STUDENT 1: OK. It's a noun. . . . Here's the first clue: "sports."

STUDENT 2: Sports? Could it be "casual"?

STUDENT 3: No, that's an adjective. It's a noun.

STUDENT 4: How about "T-shirt"?

STUDENT 1: Is that your first guess?

(Everyone agrees.)

STUDENT 1: It's not "T-shirt." OK. . . . Second clue: "feet."

STUDENT 3: What about "athletic shoes"?

(Everyone agrees.)

STUDENT 1: So "athletic shoes" is your second guess? That's right!

4 Focus on Speaking

A PRONUNCIATION: Thought Groups

When you speak, listeners will understand you better if you break longer sentences into shorter thought groups.

Rules	Examples
If you are reading aloud, pause when you see a comma or a period.	**Written:** Shanika De Silva, a native Sri Lankan, is our guest. **Spoken:** Shanika De Silva, a native Sri Lankan, is our guest.

There are no fixed rules for the length of thought groups. Many thought groups are grammatical groupings (for example, a prepositional phrase or an article + a noun). When you're learning a language, it's better to use shorter thought groups.	**Option 1:** Comfort is important,
	   but you need to look stylish.
	Option 2: Comfort is important,
	   but you need to look stylish.

1 *Read the following sentences from Listening One. Underline the thought groups.*

1. It's a long piece of cloth that's wrapped around your waist.

2. They're great for formal occasions, but if you're hanging out with friends, you want something more modern.

3. . . . family background can influence the way you dress.

4. The men, I guess, used to wear a sarong.

5. . . . when I was a kid growing up in Sri Lanka, I didn't want to wear saris.

6. But now that I'm older, I like to wear saris sometimes.

 Listen to the sentences. Check your markings. There may be some small differences between your thought groups and the thought groups on the audio program. Some differences may be fine. Some may be incorrect. Discuss any differences with the class.

2 *If you pause in the wrong place in a sentence, you can sometimes change the meaning. Match each sentence in the left column below with its meaning in the right column.*

Sentence

Meaning

1. **a.** She wore a pretty old dress.

   b. She wore a pretty, old dress.

   c. The dress was pretty and old.

   d. The dress was very old.

2. **a.** He's wearing a light blue sweater.

   b. He's wearing a light, blue sweater.

   c. The sweater isn't heavy.

   d. The color of the sweater is light blue.

3. **a.** We had chocolate, cake, and coffee after the fashion show.

   b. We had chocolate cake and coffee after the fashion show.

   c. There were two things to eat.

   d. There was one thing to eat.

4. **a.** We gave her a sweater, vest, and scarf.

   b. We gave her a sweater vest and scarf.

   c. We gave her three presents.

   d. We gave her two presents.

5. **a.** "Sally," said Paul, "hates dresses."

   b. Sally said, "Paul hates dresses."

   c. Paul hates dresses.

   d. Sally hates dresses.

6. **a.** I bought red shoes and socks.

   b. I bought red shoes, and socks.

   c. The socks are red.

   d. We don't know the color of the socks.

3 *Read the sentences in Exercise 2 with a partner. Student A reads either sentence **a** or sentence **b**. Student B listens and chooses the correct meaning, **c** or **d**. Switch roles after item 3.*

B STYLE: Introductions for Oral Presentations

When you give an oral presentation, it is important to introduce the topic before you begin talking about it. This helps to prepare the audience to listen.

Oral Presentation Suggestions	Examples
Use an attention grabber to get your audience interested.	See Unit 1, Section 4B, page 13.
State your topic. *Note:* When you state your topic, make sure that you are specific.	• Today I'd like to talk about . . . • My topic for today is . . . • Today I'd like to talk about **jeans**. (too general) • Today I'd like to talk about **how jeans have influenced the way people dress at work**. (specific)
Define any special vocabulary if necessary. *Note:* Keep your definitions simple and clear.	• A *sari* is a long piece of silky cloth that is wrapped around the body. • *Practical* means sensible and useful. • Platform shoes are shoes with elevated soles. (too difficult) • Platform shoes are shoes with thick bottoms that make you taller. (simpler)

1 *Read the list of general oral presentation topics. Choose one topic and make it more specific. Then prepare an introduction for your topic. Use the outline to help you plan.*

Oral Presentation Topics

body piercing   hairstyles   teenage fashions
brand-name clothes   men's vs. women's clothing   traditional clothing
clothing for the office sports clothing   uniforms

General topic: _____

Specific topic: _____

Outline

Introduction
Attention grabber: _____
Statement of topic: _____
Definition of important vocabulary (optional): _____
_____
Notes on other things you would like to say:
• _____
• _____
• _____

2 *Meet in small groups. Take turns presenting your introductions. After each introduction, the other students in the group will predict what ideas the rest of the presentation will include.*

C   GRAMMAR: *Used to*

1 *Read the paragraph below. Underline **used to** or **didn't use to** and the verbs that follow. Then answer the questions.*

Shanika <u>didn't use to wear</u> saris. When she was young, she used to wear jeans and other types of Western clothing. She used to feel more comfortable that way. Later, when she was older, she learned about the value of traditional clothing and started to wear saris for special occasions.

1. Look at the phrases you underlined. Why does the speaker use *used to* instead of the simple past tense?

2. In the last sentence the speaker uses the simple past instead of *used to*. Why? (*Hint:* As an adult, Shanika still understands the value of saris and continues to wear them.)

Use *used to* to talk about repeated actions, states, or habits in the past that usually don't happen anymore.

Used to	Examples
1. To make a statement with ***used to***: • Use ***used to*** + base form of verb.	Shanika **used to wear** only Western clothes, but now she sometimes wears saris.
2. To make a negative with ***used to***: • Use ***didn't***. • Remove ***d*** from ***used***.	Shanika **didn't use to wear** saris, but now she does.

2 *Work in pairs. Look at these pictures of Shanika's mother as a young woman in Sri Lanka and as an older woman in the United States. Student A begins a sentence by telling what Shanika's mother used to wear. Student B completes the sentence by telling what Shanika's mother wears now. Take turns being Student A and B.*

Example: STUDENT A: Shanika's mother used to wear dark-colored lipstick . . .

STUDENT B: . . . but now she wears light-colored lipstick.

D SPEAKING TOPIC

Impromptu presentations are talks that you give without much preparation. Making an impromptu presentation will challenge you to think quickly and will also give you practice talking in front of a group.

Read the background information about fashion trends that have changed the way we dress or look.

Some fashions come and go. People wear them for a short time and then don't wear them again. Other fashions continue for a long time, and some may even change the way people dress forever. Here is a list of fashions that have influenced the way people dress today.

athletic shoes	dyed (colored) or permed hair	nail polish
baggy pants	high heels	pants for women
baseball caps	jeans	shorts
bikinis	miniskirts	T-shirts

CHOOSING AND PRESENTING A TOPIC

Form groups of six or seven. Follow the steps below to choose and present a topic.

Step 1: Write each of the fashion trends from the list above on a separate piece of paper. Put the papers in a container.

Step 2: Student A picks a piece of paper from the container and leaves the classroom for four minutes to prepare a presentation on the topic he or she picked. (Use the outline on page 143 to prepare.)

Step 3: Student A returns. Before Student A presents, Student B picks a piece of paper and leaves to prepare.

Step 4: While Student B is preparing, Student A gives a two-minute presentation to the group. Then Student A discusses the topic with the group for one to two minutes. During the discussion, group members can talk about the Listening Task questions on page 144.

Step 5: Student B returns. Before Student B presents, Student C picks a piece of paper and leaves to prepare.

Step 6: Continue until everyone has given a presentation.

OUTLINE FOR PREPARING

When you prepare your presentation, don't write out every word. Just make brief notes in the outline on page 143. Follow these steps to complete the outline. Use your outline as a guide when you present.

Step 1: Introduction—Think of an attention grabber to interest your group in your topic (see Section 4B). Then state your topic.

Step 2: Body—Make notes to provide additional information:

1. Describe the fashion item.

2. Explain what people in your culture used to do or wear before this fashion became popular. (Remember to use the correct grammar for *used to*; see Section 4C.)

3. Explain what people in your culture do or wear now as a result of this fashion.

4. Give your opinion about this fashion. Do you like it? Why or why not?

5. Add any other comments about this fashion.

Step 3: Conclusion—Summarize your presentation in one sentence. Think of questions to begin your group discussion of the topic.

Outline

Introduction

1. Attention grabber: _____

2. Topic: _____

Body

1. Description: _____

2. Before this fashion: _____

_____

3. Results of this fashion: _____

_____

4. Opinion: _____

_____

5. Other comments: _____

_____

Conclusion

1. Summary sentence: _____

_____

2. Discussion questions: _____

_____

Listening Task

As you listen to each presentation, think of these questions:

1. How do people in your culture feel about this fashion item?

2. How do you feel about this fashion item?

Be prepared to share your thoughts during the two-minute discussion time after the presentation.

E   RESEARCH TOPICS

INTERPRETATION OF MAGAZINE PICTURES

Bring in a magazine picture of someone who dresses in a special way. For example, it could be a teenager, a movie star, a farmer, or a politician. Show the picture to the class and talk about what that person's clothes tell us about him or her. For example, the clothes could tell us the job the person does, whether he or she has a lot of money, his or her personality, and so on.

Example: STUDENT: Look at the pictures of Shanika on page 127. From the picture on the right we can guess that she works for a business. Her clothes look nice, which probably means that she has a well-paying job and that she pays attention to the way she looks. The picture on the left suggests that she is proud of her heritage, since she is wearing a sari. She probably leads a modern life but enjoys some tradition as well.

Listening Task

Listen to the other students' presentations. Do you agree or disagree with their interpretations? Be prepared to give your opinion.

PRESENTATION ON TRADITIONAL CLOTHING

Bring in an item of traditional clothing from your home culture and show it to the class. (If you don't have any traditional clothing, bring a picture.) Talk about the following:

- The name of the clothing
- Who wears it
- When it is worn
- Whether or not you wear it
- Any other interesting information

Listening Task

As each student presents, think of one question that you can ask him or her about the traditional clothing.

For Unit 8 Internet activities, visit the NorthStar Companion Website at
http://www.longman.com/northstar.

To Spank or Not to Spank?

1 Focus on the Topic

A   PREDICTING

Discuss these questions with the class.

1. Look at the picture. Why do you think the parent is spanking the child? What did the child do? Do you think corporal punishment* is a good punishment in this case?

2. Read the title of the unit. What do you think this unit will be about?

---

* *corporal punishment:* punishment by hitting or spanking

B   SHARING INFORMATION

Discuss these questions in small groups. Then share your ideas with the class.

1. How did your parents punish you when you were younger? How did you feel about the punishment then?

2. As a child, how did you learn right from wrong?

C   PREPARING TO LISTEN

BACKGROUND

How much do you know about corporal punishment? Take this quiz to find out.

1 *Choose a, b, or c to complete the statements.*

1. Sweden, Israel, and the United Kingdom have _____ corporal punishment of children.
   a. no laws about
   b. laws that allow
   c. laws against

2. The American Academy of Pediatrics* _____ corporal punishment.
   a. strongly supports
   b. has no opinion about
   c. strongly opposes

3. In 1950, 99% of parents in the United States said they used corporal punishment. Today, _____ say they use corporal punishment.
   a. 97%
   b. 85%
   c. 62%

4. Of parents who use corporal punishment in the United States, 80% say that it is _____.
   a. not the best form of punishment
   b. the only form of punishment they use
   c. the most effective type of punishment

2 *Check your answers in Student Activities on page 185. Then discuss these questions.*

1. Which answers did you get right? Which did you get wrong?

2. Which answers surprised you? Why?

---

pediatrics: the area of medicine that deals with children and their health

VOCABULARY FOR COMPREHENSION

Read this letter to a newspaper advice column. Then match each underlined word or phrase with the correct definition. Write the number in the blank.

City Herald   Monday, September 8

Gabby van Anders

Dear Gabby,

My husband and I disagree about how to **(1)** <u>discipline</u> our children. We have different ideas about how to punish them when they **(2)** <u>misbehave</u>, or do something bad. He thinks spanking is **(3)** <u>acceptable</u>. He says that we should do it **(4)** <u>for their own good</u>, so our children will learn right and wrong. He wants our children to **(5)** <u>respect</u> us and listen to what we say.

I'm against spanking. I **(6)** <u>admit</u> that I sometimes feel like hitting my children when I am very angry, but I think it's wrong. Spanking is a form of **(7)** <u>violence</u>. It is a form of **(8)** <u>child abuse</u> and is very harmful to children. In my opinion, spanking children should be against the law. Spanking can **(9)** <u>lead to</u> more serious problems. When kids **(10)** <u>get in trouble</u>, we need to talk to them and find out about the problem, not spank them.

My husband and I have a lot of arguments about this. He **(11)** <u>complains</u> that I do not really punish the kids. I think he abuses them. How can we solve this problem?

Signed,
Confused Mom

_____ **a.** to have a good opinion of someone

_____ **b.** bad or cruel treatment of a child

_____ **c.** in order to help them

_____ **d.** to say that you are unhappy about something

_____ **e.** to punish someone

_____ **f.** to get caught doing something wrong

_____ **g.** to make something happen

_____ **h.** thought to be all right by most people

_____ **i.** to unwillingly say that something about yourself is true

_____ **j.** behavior that hurts someone in a physical way

_____ **k.** to behave badly

2 Focus on Listening

A   LISTENING ONE: *A Radio Report*

 Listen to an excerpt of a radio report. Answer the questions.

1. What opinion do you think will be presented in the report? Why?

_____ Supporting spanking (thinking it's good)

_____ Opposing spanking (thinking it's bad)

_____ Both opinions

2. The reporter interviews several different people. Who do you think will give an opinion about spanking? Why?

_____ Police officer   _____ Child

_____ Doctor   _____ Teacher

_____ Parent

LISTENING FOR MAIN IDEAS

 Listen to the report. Do the people being interviewed support spanking or oppose spanking? Check (✓) each person's opinion. Write at least one reason for each opinion.

SPEAKER	SUPPORTS	OPPOSES	REASON(S)
1. Rhonda Moore	☐	☐	
2. Taylor Robinson	☐	☐	
3. Dr. John Oparah	☐	☐	
4. Dr. Beverly Lau	☐	☐	

LISTENING FOR DETAILS

 *Listen again to all the opinions and reasons the speakers give. What does each speaker believe about spanking? Write **Y** (yes) if the statement expresses the speaker's beliefs. Write **N** (no) if the statement does not express the speaker's beliefs.*

Rhonda Moore, parent

—————— **1.** Pain helps children learn right and wrong.

—————— **2.** Spanking is done out of anger.

—————— **3.** Her children don't understand why they are spanked.

Taylor Robinson, parent

—————— **4.** Spanking teaches children to solve problems with violence.

—————— **5.** Spanking teaches children to talk about problems.

Dr. John Oparah, doctor

—————— **6.** Many children don't respect their parents.

—————— **7.** Parents who spank should be treated like criminals.

—————— **8.** Some parents are afraid their children will call the police.

Dr. Beverly Lau, doctor

—————— **9.** Children who are spanked misbehave less often.

REACTING TO THE LISTENING

 1 *People use their words and tone of voice to show how strongly they feel about their opinions. Listen to excerpts and decide how strongly each speaker feels. Circle the number in the chart on page 150 that best describes how the speaker feels (**1** = not strongly, **5** = very strongly). Then note the words or tone of voice that helped you understand the speaker's feelings.*

EXCERPT	NOT STRONGLY		VERY STRONGLY			WORDS OR TONE OF VOICE
1. Rhonda Moore	1	2	3	4	5	
2. Taylor Robinson	1	2	3	4	5	
3. Dr. John Oparah	1	2	3	4	5	
4. Dr. Beverly Lau	1	2	3	4	5	

Compare your answers with the class. Which speaker had the strongest feelings about his or her opinion? How can you tell?

2 *Discuss these questions in small groups.*

1. Do you support or oppose spanking as a form of punishment? Why?

2. What are some other effective ways to discipline a child?

B LISTENING TWO: *Expert Opinions*

What are the effects of spanking as children get older and become adults? Listen to three people's opinions about the long-term effects of spanking. Check (✓) whether the speaker supports or opposes spanking. Then listen again and write the reasons for each speaker's opinion.

SPEAKER	SUPPORTS	OPPOSES	REASON(S)
1. Donald Sterling	❏	❏	
2. Dr. Phyllis Jones	❏	❏	
3. Lois Goldin	❏	❏	

C   LINKING LISTENINGS ONE AND TWO

In small groups, review the reasons that the speakers in Listening One and Listening Two support or oppose spanking. (The reasons are listed in the charts on pages 148 and 150.) Make a list of the two most convincing opinions from each side. Discuss with your classmates why you think they are the strongest arguments.

3 Focus on Vocabulary

1 *Cross out the word or phrase below each sentence that has a different meaning from the underlined word or phrase. Use a dictionary to look up words you don't know.*

1. I was very **angry at** my son when he broke the window.
   - upset with
   - pleased with

2. Sometimes I **spank** my children when they do something wrong.
   - yell at
   - hit

3. I don't **support** parents who spank their children.
   - agree with
   - reward

4. Spanking **leads to** other problems.
   - prevents
   - causes

5. My daughter **admitted** that she had broken the window.
   - told me
   - denied

6. In some places, it is **acceptable** for teachers to hit their students.
   - all right
   - wrong

7. Some parents **punish** their children by spanking.
   - reward
   - discipline

8. I think spanking is a form of **abuse**.
   - love
   - violence

9. My children **complain about** their punishment if they don't like it.
   - oppose
   - agree to

10. All children **misbehave** in school sometimes.
    - do well
    - get in trouble

2 *Work in pairs. Use the vocabulary from the list below to make statements supporting and opposing corporal punishment. Student A uses the first word or phrase to make a sentence supporting corporal punishment. Then Student B makes an opposing sentence using the same vocabulary word. Continue through the list. Switch roles after number 7.*

Example: STUDENT A: Spanking is a useful way to *discipline* children. Children remember when you spank them.

STUDENT B: No, it is better to *discipline* in other ways; for example, sending a child to his room.

1. discipline
2. misbehave
3. acceptable
4. for their own good
5. respect
6. spanking
7. angry

8. admit
9. child abuse
10. violence
11. lead to
12. arrest
13. get in trouble
14. complain

4 Focus on Speaking

A   PRONUNCIATION: Final Consonants

Sometimes it is difficult to say and hear the difference between the sounds /z/ and /s/ at the ends of words.

Explanation	Examples		
/z/ is a *voiced* consonant. The vocal chords vibrate (move back and forth) when you say this sound.	**raise**	**prize**	**faze**
/s/ is a *voiceless* consonant. The vocal chords don't vibrate.	**race**	**price**	**face**
Note: Some nouns and verbs are spelled the same, but pronounced differently. • The verbs end in the /z/ sound. • The nouns end in the /s/ sound.	**to abuse** **child abuse**	**to excuse** **a bad excuse**	**to use** **a good use**

1 *Listen to the final sounds in the underlined words. Put a check (✓) next to the sound you hear.*

1. He asked the counselor to <u>advise</u> him.

    "Advise"   _____ /s/   _____ /z/

2. The counselor gave him some <u>advice</u>.

    "Advice"   _____ /s/   _____ /z/

2 *Try to say /z/ and /s/. Put four fingers along the side of your throat. Say "zzzzzzzz." What do you feel? Then say "sssssss." What do you feel?*

3 *Listen to the words and repeat them.*

/z/	/s/
abuse (verb)	abuse (noun)
lose	loose
peas	piece/peace
eyes	ice
fears	fierce
rise	rice
plays	place
knees	niece
advise	advice
raise	race

4 *Listen again. You will hear one word from each pair above. Circle the word you hear. Check your answers with the class.*

5 *Work with a partner. Take turns saying a word from each of the pairs in the list above to your partner. Your partner will repeat the word and point to either /z/ or /s/.*

6 *Listen to the following tongue twisters and repeat.*

1. The advisor gave them some advice to raise race horses.

2. Did the police abuse Dale Clover's rights when they arrested him for child abuse?

3. My niece hurt her knees, so I placed some frozen peas on them.

4. My son fears that our neighbor's fierce dog will lose his collar and get loose.

Choose one of the tongue twisters, practice it, and say it to the class.

7 *Work in pairs. Student A reads either sentence **a** or sentence **b** from item 1 in the left column. Student B listens and chooses the correct response, either sentence **c** or sentence **d**. Continue through the list. Then switch roles and repeat.*

Sentence	Response
1. a. Did you get a good price?	**c.** Yes, it was very cheap.
b. Did you get a good prize?	**d.** Yes, I came in first.
2. a. Do you want peas?	**c.** No, I don't like them.
b. Do you want peace?	**d.** Yes, for the whole world.
3. a. I have blue ice.	**c.** How did you make it blue?
b. I have blue eyes.	**d.** Does your mother have them too?
4. a. I asked him for a raise.	**c.** Did you get the money?
b. I asked him for a race.	**d.** Who won?

B   STYLE: Supporting Your Opinions

If you want to persuade someone to agree with you, it is necessary to support, or explain, your opinions. Look at four common ways to support your opinions.

1. Give **facts** to show that your ideas are based on true information, not just on feelings.

    Spanking helps to prevent crime, not increase it. The reason for my opinion is the fact that crime has increased as spanking has decreased. In the 1950s, for example, spanking was a more common form of punishment than it is today. And in the 1950s, the crime rate was lower than it is today.

2. Give **numbers or statistics** to show that your ideas are based on research.

    I strongly oppose spanking because it can turn into child abuse. I say this because 85 percent of child abuse cases start when the parent disciplines the child using corporal punishment.

3. Use **examples** to explain what you are talking about.

    I don't think spanking teaches children anything. Let me give you an example. What if a child hits his friend and is then spanked as punishment? He may be very confused about when hitting is bad and when it's O.K.

4. Tell a **personal story** to show that your ideas are based on experience.

    I think spanking helps children learn. For instance, I once stole some candy from the store. My father spanked me when he found out. I always remembered that spanking, and I never stole anything again.

There are many phrases that you can use to introduce support:

For example, . . .   I say this because . . .

For instance, . . .   The reason for my opinion is that . . .

Let me give you an example.

Read the two discussion topics below. Circle "Agree" or "Disagree" to show your opinion. Then write a fact, statistic, personal story, or example to support your opinion.

Discussion Topics

1. Parents should spank their children as a form of discipline.   Agree / Disagree

   Support: _____

   _____

2. Teachers should spank their students as a form of discipline.   Agree / Disagree

   Support: _____

   _____

In small groups, discuss each topic for five minutes. Use your notes to help support your opinions. Then report on your discussion to the class. What types of support did your classmates give? Which support was the most persuasive? Why?

C   GRAMMAR: Present Perfect Tense

1 *Read the paragraph and answer the questions below. Notice the italicized verbs in the present perfect tense.*

The number of parents in the United States who spank their children *has decreased* in the past fifty years. Public opinion about spanking *has changed*. Many doctors *have said* that spanking is harmful—or is even a form of child abuse. Parents *have learned* new ways to discipline their children. However, at the same time, the number of crimes committed by children *has not gone* down, it *has increased*.

1. How is the present perfect tense formed?

2. When do we use the present perfect tense?

3. When do we use the simple past tense?

Present Perfect Tense	Examples
Use the present perfect: • to talk about things that happened at an unspecified time in the past. • to talk about things that started in the past, continue in the present, and may continue into the future.	Many doctors **have said** that spanking is harmful. (We don't know *when* they said this.) The number of parents who spank their children **has decreased** in the past 100 years. (The number started decreasing in the past and will probably continue to decrease.)
To form the present perfect, use **have / has** + the **past participle.** **Have** and **has** are usually contracted in informal speech.	Public opinion about spanking **has changed**. People **have learned** new ways to discipline their children. He**'s changed** his opinion about spanking.
To form a negative, add **not** after **have / has**.	The number of crimes **has not gone** down.
To form *yes/no* questions, begin with **have / has**. To form **wh-** questions, begin with a **wh-** word.	**Have** you **read** the report about spanking? **Why have** you **stopped** spanking your child?

2 *In the United States, beliefs about spanking and discipline have changed in the last 50 years. Complete these statements using the present perfect tense. Compare your answers in small groups.*

1. Parents' beliefs about spanking _____ (*change*) in the United States. Many parents _____ (*stop*) using spanking as their most important method of discipline.

2. The United States government _____ (*pass*) stronger laws against child abuse. Police _____ (*arrest*) more parents for abusing their children.

3. Many American doctors _____ (*advise*) parents not
   to spank their children. They _____ (*suggest*) using
   nonviolent methods of discipline.

4. The number of crimes committed by children and teenagers
   _____ (*rise*) in the United States. Some people believe
   that this is because parents _____ (*not / teach*) their
   children the difference between right and wrong.

5. American teachers _____ (*stop*) using
   corporal punishment in the classroom. The government
   _____ (*decide*) that it is against the law for
   teachers to hit their students.

3 *Work in small groups. Complete the following questions with the present perfect. Then
take turns asking and answering the questions to discuss how beliefs have changed in
other cultures. Answer about a culture with which you are familiar (not the United
States).*

   Example: STUDENT A: How *have* parents' beliefs about discipline *changed*?

   STUDENT B: In Turkey, parents now feel . . .

   STUDENT C: Japan is different from Turkey. Parents in Japan think . . .

1. How _____ parents' beliefs about discipline
   _____ (*change*)?

2. What kind of laws against child abuse _____ the government
   _____ (*pass*)?

3. How _____ doctors _____ (*advise*) parents to
   discipline their children?

4. _____ the number of crimes committed by children
   _____ (*rise*) or _____ (*fall*)?

5. How _____ discipline in schools _____
   (*change*)?

D SPEAKING TOPIC

In a debate, two teams discuss different sides of the same topic. One team is **For** (supporting) an opinion about the topic. The other team is **Against** (opposing) the opinion.

Work in two teams. You will debate an opinion related to punishment. (If you have a large class, you may divide into groups and have several debates on different topics.)

CHOOSING A TOPIC

Read the topics below and the background information that follows each topic. Choose a topic to debate. Decide which team will be ***For*** *and which will be* ***Against*** *the opinion.*

Topics

1. Parents using spanking to discipline their children

   Some countries have passed laws that say it is wrong for parents to hit or spank their children. In other countries, parents can punish their children however they want.

2. Teachers using spanking to discipline their students

   In some countries, teachers can hit or spank their students when the students misbehave. In other countries, it is against the law for teachers to hit their students.

3. Governments using corporal punishment to punish criminals

   In some countries, the government uses corporal punishment (hitting or beating) to punish criminals. In other countries, the government can't use corporal punishment.

4. Punishing parents when their children do something wrong

   In the United States, some people want to pass a new law that says if a child under 18 does something wrong (such as stealing from a store or missing school), the parents will be punished because they did not control their child.

PREPARING

Each team will work together to plan the debate. You will plan what to say in support of your opinion and how to argue against the other team. There are three steps to planning the debate:

Step 1: Explain and defend your team's ideas.

- Think of three main points, or arguments, to support your opinion. Support your points with facts, statistics, examples, and personal stories (see Section 4B).

- Think of arguments the other team might make against your main points. Decide what to say to defend your ideas or to show that your ideas are correct.

- Outline each of your points, following the pattern below.

  I. Main point

     A. Support for point

     B. Possible argument(s) against point

       1. Ways to defend point

Step 2: Prepare to speak against the other team.

- Think of three possible main points that the other team will make to support their opinion.

- Decide what you will say to show that the other team is wrong.

- Outline each possible point following the pattern below.

  I. Other team's main point

     A. Arguments to show they are wrong

Step 3: Divide the speaking tasks. Each team member will talk during the debate. Decide which team member will explain each part of the debate.

DEBATING

Follow the steps below.

Step 1: *For* team explains its first point.

Step 2: *Against* team members discuss briefly among themselves and then argue against *For* team's point.

Step 3: *Against* team explains its first point.

Step 4: *For* team members discuss briefly among themselves and then argue against *Against* team's point.

Step 5: *For* team explains its second point, and so on. Continue until both teams make their main points.

E   RESEARCH TOPIC

OBSERVATION

Step 1: Visit a place where you can see adults taking care of young children. For example, visit a nursery school or preschool, go to a playground, or visit a friend or relative who has children. Watch the children and adults for an hour or so. Look for times when a child misbehaves and an adult disciplines the child. Use the chart to take notes about what you see.

WHY DID THE ADULTS DISCIPLINE THE CHILDREN?	HOW DID THE ADULTS DISCIPLINE THE CHILD(REN)?	WAS IT EFFECTIVE?
A child threw something at another child.	An adult yelled and told the child not to throw things.	No.

Here are some things an adult may do to discipline a child (also look for other things that are not on this list):

- Say "No" to the child.

- Take something away from the child.

- Move the child to a different place.

- Make the child sit by himself or herself.

- Hold the child so he or she can't do something.

- Yell at the child in a loud voice.

- Hit or spank the child.

Step 2: Make a tape recording of your observations. Answer these questions about what you saw.

1. What types of discipline did you see? Was the discipline violent or nonviolent?

2. Did the discipline make the child stop misbehaving? Why or why not?

3. What does this type of discipline teach a child?

4. How was the discipline the same or different from other types of discipline you have seen or experienced?

Step 3: Give the tape to your teacher for feedback.

Step 4: Discuss your observations with the class.

For Unit 9 Internet activities, visit the NorthStar Companion Website at http://www.longman.com/northstar.

Before You Say "I Do"

1 Focus on the Topic

A PREDICTING

Discuss these questions with the class.

1. What's happening in the picture?

2. When do people say "I do" in a wedding?

3. How can a couple make sure they will have a happy marriage?

B SHARING INFORMATION

Work in small groups. Read the quotations about marriage. After each quotation is a sentence that summarizes the quotation. Circle the best answer to complete each sentence.

1. "In almost every marriage, there is a selfish and an unselfish partner. A pattern begins and never changes, of one person always asking for something and the other person always giving something away."
   —Adapted from Iris Murdoch, British writer and philosopher (1919–1999)

   In most marriages, _____ can get what he or she wants.
   a. only one person
   b. both the husband and wife
   c. neither the husband nor the wife (no one)

2. "A man who is a good friend is likely to find a good wife because marriage is based on a talent for friendship."
   —Adapted from Friedrich Nietzsche, German philosopher (1844–1900)

   To have a happy marriage, a man must _____.
   a. have a good friend
   b. be a good friend to his wife
   c. be sure his wife has a good friend

3. "Keep your eyes wide open before marriage, and half shut afterwards."
   —Benjamin Franklin, American statesman and philosopher (1701–1790)

   Choose your husband or wife carefully, but _____ after marriage.
   a. ignore your spouse's* mistakes
   b. try to change your spouse
   c. don't look at your spouse

Discuss the quotations with the class. Do you agree or disagree with the writers? Why or why not?

C PREPARING TO LISTEN

BACKGROUND

A prenuptial† agreement is a written agreement between two people who are going to get married. Most prenuptial agreements describe what will happen to a couple's money, property, or children if the marriage ends in divorce.

Some prenuptial agreements also describe how the husband and wife must act during the marriage. Steve and Karen Parsons made a very unusual prenuptial

---

*spouse: husband or wife
†prenuptial: before marriage [pronounced pre-nəp-shəl]

agreement. Instead of talking about what would happen if the marriage ended, the agreement stated rules for almost every part of their daily lives.

Legal experts agree that this agreement probably cannot be enforced in a court of law. However, the husband and wife have both agreed to follow the rules described in the agreement.

1 *Read the following excerpts from Steve and Karen's prenuptial agreement.*

Prenuptial Agreement
Steve and Karen Parsons

1. Daily Habits
1.1. On weekdays we will go to sleep by 11 P.M. and wake up by 6:00 A.M. On weekends we will go to sleep by 1 A.M. and wake up before 10 A.M.
1.2. We will not drive over the speed limit and will always wear our seatbelts.
1.3. We will eat healthy food that is low in fat and sugar. We will not gain more than 10 pounds over our weight on our wedding day.

2. Household Chores
2.1. We agree to share the household chores. Karen will take care of meals and cleaning inside the house. Steve will do repairs and take care of the garden.
2.2. We will both do the laundry. Steve will wash and dry the clothes, and Karen will fold them and put them away. We will put the dirty clothes in the laundry bag, not on the floor.
2.3. We will both make a list of groceries every week. Karen will do the shopping. She will buy only the items on the list and will try to buy things on sale.

3. Communication
3.1. We will spend at least 15–30 minutes each day talking to each other and not doing anything else.
3.2. If we are angry, we will not yell or call each other names. We will go into another room until we don't feel angry anymore.
3.3. If we want to change a rule in this agreement, we will talk about it until we can find a solution we both agree on.

4. Children
4.1. We will wait for two years before we have a child. We will have two children.
4.2. After our first child is born, the partner who makes less money will quit his/her job and stay home with the child.

---

2 *Discuss these questions with the class.*

1. Which rules in the prenuptial agreement do you agree with? Which rules do you disagree with? Why?

2. Do you think this type of prenuptial agreement is a good idea? Why or why not?

VOCABULARY FOR COMPREHENSION

Match each underlined word with its definition below. Write the correct number in the blank.

Yoko's Problem

After we got married, I found out that my husband and I had different (**1**) <u>expectations</u> about marriage. He wanted me to do all the cleaning, while I thought that we should share it. Before we were married, he lived by himself and cleaned his own apartment. So it (**2**) <u>bothered</u> me that suddenly, after we married, he didn't want to do any cleaning! Fortunately, we were able to (**3**) <u>work out</u> the problem. We sat down and talked. We both explained our point of view. Then we reached a (**4**) <u>compromise</u>. We both agreed to cook dinner three times a week. We also divided the cleaning chores in half. We had to (**5**) <u>spend a lot of time</u> talking, but we finally agreed on something that made us both happy.

_____   **a.** annoyed

_____   **b.** agreement

_____   **c.** beliefs or hopes that something will happen

_____   **d.** use or take a lot of time

_____   **e.** solve

Lorenzo's Problem

Some of the arguments my wife and I have (**6**) <u>concern</u> little things. For example, my wife has one (**7**) <u>quirk</u> that I don't like. I love to play games, such as cards, Monopoly, and Scrabble. However, whenever we play a game, my wife likes to (**8**) <u>break the rules</u>. She says it is more fun to change the rules and play in a different way. I don't agree. Many arguments between us (**9**) <u>occur</u> because of this problem. I always have to (**10**) <u>check on</u> her to make sure she is following the rules.

_____   **f.** not obey the rules

_____   **g.** watch

_____   **h.** are about

_____   **i.** happen

_____   **j.** strange habit

2 Focus on Listening

A LISTENING ONE: *A Prenuptial Agreement*

 You will hear an interview with Steve and Karen Parsons about their prenuptial agreement. Listen to the beginning of the interview. Then read some questions the reporter could ask Steve and Karen. How do you think they would answer the questions? Write your predictions below.

1. Possible question: Steve, Karen, first I'd like to ask you why you decided to write this unusual agreement?

   Predicted answer: _____

   _____

2. Possible question: So do you spend a lot of time checking on each other to see if the rules are being followed?

   Predicted answer: _____

   _____

3. Possible question: Do you think other couples should follow your example and write prenuptial agreements of their own?

   Predicted answer: _____

   _____

LISTENING FOR MAIN IDEAS

Listen to the interview. Steve and Karen are discussing several problems that married people have. Put a check (✓) next to the four problems that are mentioned in the interview.

_____ 1. Different expectations

_____ 2. Problems with other family members

_____ 3. Not respecting each other's quirks

_____ 4. Arguments about pets

_____ 5. Not talking about what each person wants

_____ 6. Disagreements about money

_____ 7. Jealousy* about other men/women

---

* *jealousy:* the feeling of being angry because someone you love is paying too much attention to someone else

LISTENING FOR DETAILS

*Listen again. Decide if each statement is **T** (true) or **F** (false).*

_____ 1. Steve and Karen have a five-page prenuptial agreement.

_____ 2. Both Steve and Karen have been married before.

_____ 3. It bothered Steve when his ex-wife left her clothes lying on the floor.

_____ 4. Karen says that the prenuptial agreement is like a business contract.

_____ 5. Karen thinks that working out a compromise is more romantic than flowers and candy.

_____ 6. Steve and Karen feel that they spend the same amount of time arguing as other couples do.

_____ 7. Steve and Karen agree about all the rules in the prenuptial agreement.

_____ 8. Steve and Karen feel that a prenuptial agreement could be useful for other couples.

REACTING TO THE LISTENING

1 *Listen to three excerpts from the interview with Steve and Karen. Then read the following summaries of the quotations in Section 1B. Would Steve and Karen agree with the ideas in each summary? Check **Yes** or **No**. Write down words or phrases from the listening that help support your answer.*

Excerpt 1

The quote by Iris Murdoch says that in most marriages only one person can get what he or she wants.

Would Steve and Karen agree with this idea?   ❑ Yes   ❑ No

Words or phrases to support your answer: _____

_____

Excerpt 2

The quote by Friedrich Nietzsche says that to have a happy marriage, a man must be a good friend to his wife.

Would Steve and Karen agree with this idea?   ❑ Yes   ❑ No

Words or phrases to support your answer: _____

_____

Excerpt 3

The quote by Benjamin Franklin says that you should choose your spouse carefully but ignore his or her mistakes after marriage.

Would Steve and Karen agree with this idea?   ❑ Yes   ❑ No

Words or phrases to support your answer: _____

_____

Compare your answers in small groups. Why would Steve and Karen agree or disagree with each quote? Give examples from the listening to explain your answer.

2 *Do you agree or disagree with Steve and Karen's opinions about marriage? Work individually to make a list of the ideas that you agree and disagree with. Then work in small groups to compare your opinions and discuss.*

3 *What would you say if your fiancé/fiancée* asked you to write a prenuptial agreement like Steve and Karen's? Compare your answers in small groups.*

B   LISTENING TWO: *Reactions to the Prenuptial Agreement*

 Listen to people's reactions to Steve and Karen's prenuptial agreement. Do they think the agreement is a good idea or a bad idea? Check (✓) the appropriate box according to each speaker's opinion. Then match each speaker with the reason for his or her opinion. Write the letter for the reason in the chart.

	GOOD IDEA	BAD IDEA	REASON
Speaker 1	❑	❑	
Speaker 2	❑	❑	
Speaker 3	❑	❑	
Speaker 4	❑	❑	
Speaker 5	❑	❑	

Reason

a. Helps couples talk about problems

b. Makes couples think carefully before they marry

c. Not romantic

d. Too many details

e. Not legal

_____

**fiancé / fiancée:* the man/woman you are going to marry

C   LINKING LISTENINGS ONE AND TWO

1 *Work in pairs. Combine the ideas in Listenings One and Two to write a list of arguments* **for** *and* **against** *prenuptial agreements.*

Arguments *for* prenuptial agreements

1. _____

2. _____

3. _____

4. _____

Arguments *against* prenuptial agreements

1. _____

2. _____

3. _____

4. _____

2 *Circle the strongest* **for** *and* **against** *arguments. Explain to the class why you think these are the strongest arguments.*

3 Focus on Vocabulary

1 *Make words from the scrambled letters. Write one letter in each square. Don't worry yet about the numbers below the boxes. You will use them in the next exercise.*

1. It really TEBSOHR me when people talk in a movie theater.

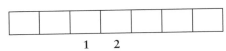

2. When my husband and I have a problem, we KOWR TOU a solution we both agree on.

3. My husband wanted to go to the mountains and I wanted to go to a lake. So we found a SOORMCMPIE and went to the ocean instead.

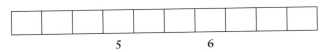

4. Arguments CORCU when two people don't agree about something.

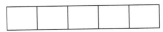

5. I think a prenuptial GEETENMAR is a good idea.

       8

6. You will get a ticket if you BERKA the traffic rules.

       9

7. Let's KECHC NO the baby to make sure he is all right.

  10

8. Most arguments between my wife and me NOCRECN money.

     11

9. My parents and I have different SOITEPXANCET about who I will marry.

           12   13

10. My wife has a few SKUIRQ, such as singing in the shower.

   14   15

11. My spouse and I like to SENDP IMET having fun, not arguing.

   16

12. The Parsons' prenuptial agreement probably doesn't have any LALGE power in court.

   17

2 *Figure out the saying about marriage. Copy the letters in the numbered squares from Exercise 1 to the squares below with the same numbers.*

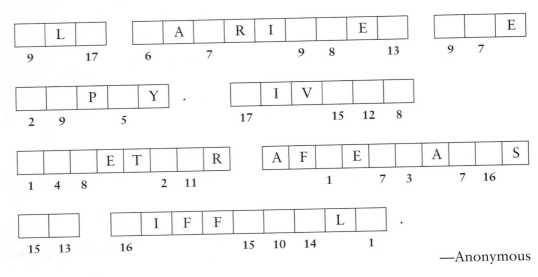

—Anonymous

Discuss with the class whether you agree with this saying.

3 *Work in small groups to create a role play.*

1. Write each word or phrase from the word box on a small piece of paper. Fold the papers and mix them together in a container.

agreement	check on	disagree	occur	romantic
bother	compromise	expectation	quirk	spend time
break a rule	concern	legal	respect	work out

2. Pick three pieces of paper and read them as a group. Do not show them to the class.

3. Choose a situation from the list below. As a group, write a role play about the situation. Use the three vocabulary words you picked in your role play.

Situations

- Parents and other family members are talking to their son or daughter about his or her plans for marriage.

- Friends are discussing who they want to marry.

- Friends are trying to find dates using the Internet.

- Roommates or members of a family are deciding who should do the cooking, cleaning, shopping, and so on for the group.

- Your choice

4. Practice the role play and then perform it for the class.

Listening Task

As you watch the role plays by the other groups, listen carefully for the three vocabulary words they use. Write them down. When the role play is finished, tell the class which words you wrote down.

4 Focus on Speaking

A PRONUNCIATION: Contrastive Stress

When we speak, we usually stress content words (nouns, verbs, adjectives, and adverbs). However, when we introduce new information into a conversation, we often emphasize different words to show that the new information contrasts with, or is different from, the old information. This kind of emphasis is called contrastive stress. By emphasizing, or highlighting, different words in a sentence, you can change the meaning.

Word Stress	Examples
Normal Sentence Stress Stress content words: • Nouns • Verbs • Adjectives • Adverbs	I **usually wash** the **dishes**.
Contrastive Stress Stress words that add new information or contradict previous information.	**I** usually wash the dishes. (Not my wife.) I usually **wash** the dishes. (Not dry them.) I usually wash the **dishes**. (Not the car.)
To emphasize a word, say the word. • Higher in pitch (tone) • Louder • Longer	**He** does the shopping. **HE** does the shopping. **H-e-e** does the shopping.

1 *Listen to the following sentences. Underline the word that is emphasized. Then circle* ***a*** *or* ***b*** *to choose the meaning of the sentence.*

1. <u>Karen</u> will do the grocery shopping.
   (a.) not Steve   **b.** not the laundry

2. Karen will always use a shopping list.
   a. not Steve   **b.** not sometimes

3. Nothing will be left on the floor in the bedroom.
   a. not the table   **b.** not the living room

4. On weekdays, we will go to bed at 11:00.
   a. not weekends   **b.** not at 9:00.

5. We will wait three years before buying a house.
   a. not two years   **b.** not a car

6. Karen will make a list of groceries every week.
   a. not Steve   **b.** not whenever we remember

7. We will spend at least 15 minutes a day talking with each other.
   a. not less than 15 minutes   **b.** not our relatives

8. Steve will figure out directions before we start a trip.
   a. not Karen   **b.** not after we start

9. We will eat healthy food that's low in fat and sugar.
   a. not junk food   **b.** both fat and sugar

10. We will update this agreement every year.
    a. not our lawyers   **b.** not every two years

2 *Work in pairs. Student A says the sentences from Exercise 1, using word stress to show either meaning* ***a*** *or meaning* ***b***. *Student B listens and guesses the meaning of the sentences. Then switch roles and repeat.*

Example: Karen will do the grocery shopping.

   a. not Steve   **b.** not the laundry

   STUDENT A: **Karen** will do the grocery shopping.

   STUDENT B: That means "not Steve," right?

   STUDENT A: Yes.

3 *Work in pairs. Each of the following sentences has two sets of words that are contrasted with each other. Read the sentences and circle the first set of words that are contrasted. Then underline the second set. Take turns reading the sentences aloud, using contrastive stress.*

1. (Steve's) been married <u>twice</u>, and (Karen's) been married <u>once</u>.

2. Many of the rules deal with money; only a few deal with other situations.

3. Steve takes care of the car and Karen does the housework.

4. Getting married is easy; living together afterward is more difficult.

5. On weekends, Karen gets up early and Steve gets up late.

6. When it comes to food, Steve likes Japanese and Karen likes Mexican.

7. One couple got marriage counseling, while the other couple got a divorce.

8. Most couples make verbal agreements; only a few want written agreements.

B STYLE: Interrupting Politely

To begin talking in a group discussion or conversation, you don't have to wait for permission to speak. You can politely interrupt other speakers and state your opinion or idea.

There are several reasons why a person might interrupt a conversation or discussion:

- To agree or disagree and explain why

- To ask someone to explain

- To ask someone to repeat

It is important to interrupt at the appropriate time:

- When a speaker has finished his or her sentence

- When a speaker pauses in the middle of a sentence

There are different ways to interrupt. To interrupt politely you can use one or more of the following strategies.

Body Language (Sounds and Gestures)	Words/ Phrases
Clear your throat (say "uhmm").	Excuse me, . . .
Raise your hand.	I'm sorry, . . .
Raise your index finger.	Maybe so, but . . .
Make eye contact with the speaker.	Sorry to interrupt, but . . .

1 *Work in small groups. Choose one of the following discussion topics. Take a few minutes to write down your ideas about the topic.*

- What things you should know about someone before you decide to get married or live together?

- Should people live together before they get married?

2 *As a group, discuss your topic for four minutes. Each person should interrupt at least once to agree or disagree, or to ask someone to explain or repeat. Use one of the strategies listed on page 175.*

As the group discusses, one student listens and uses the Interruption Check Sheet below to mark how each person interrupts. Each time a student interrupts, the listener puts a check (✓) in the appropriate column. At the end of the discussion, the listener shows the sheet to the group.

Interruption Check Sheet

	Name of Student	Sounds/Gestures	Words
1.	Toby	✓✓	✓
2.			
3.			
4.			

C GRAMMAR: Articles

There are three articles: a, an, *and* the. *Read the following continuation of Steve and Karen's agreement and underline the articles. Then answer the questions on page 177.*

5. Vacations
   5.1. We will take a vacation every year.
   5.2. Most of the vacations will be in the United States. Once every five years, we will take an international trip.
   5.3. We will take turns planning the vacations. The person who plans a vacation will make the travel arrangements.

1. Look at the words that follow each article. Are they verbs, nouns, adjectives, or adverbs?

2. What is the difference between *a, an,* and *the*?

Articles are small words that come before nouns or adjectives with nouns. They give information about whether a noun is specific or unspecific.

Articles	Examples
The is a definite (specific) article. Use ***the*** when:	
• You and your listener both know which noun you are talking about	Steve broke **the** rule about asking for directions while driving. (We know which rule he broke.)
• The noun is unique (there's only one)	Steve and Karen think that love is the only thing in **the** world that matters. (There's only one world.)
• The noun has been mentioned already	Steve and Karen wrote a prenuptial agreement. **The** agreement outlines each person's responsibilities. (We say "the agreement" because "agreement" was already mentioned in the first sentence.)
A / an are indefinite (unspecific) articles. Use **a / an** when:	
• The noun is singular and	Karen will use **a** shopping list when she goes grocery shopping. (We are talking about shopping lists in general, not a particular shopping list.)
• Either you or your listener do not have a particular noun in mind *Note:* Use *a* before nouns that begin with a consonant sound and *an* before nouns that begin with a vowel sound.	Steve and Karen wrote **an** agreement.

2 *Changing an article can change the meaning of a sentence. Match each sentence in the left column below with its meaning in the right column.*

Sentence

1. a. Steve wants the car.

   b. Steve wants a car.

Meaning

   c. Steve hasn't decided which car to buy.

   d. Steve wants the car that he saw in the newspaper.

2. a. Karen mailed a package.

   b. Karen mailed the package.

   c. I know which package she's mailing.

   d. I don't know which package she's mailing.

3. a. Steve and Karen went to the movie on their anniversary.

   b. Steve and Karen went to a movie on their anniversary.

   c. The movie was *Romeo and Juliet.*

   d. I don't know the title of the movie.

4. a. Steve and Karen are going to the wedding.

   b. Steve and Karen are going to the wedding.

   c. I know who's getting married.

   d. I don't know who's getting married.

5. a. Karen bought Steve the shirt for his birthday.

   b. Karen bought Steve a shirt for his birthday.

   c. I don't know what kind it was.

   d. It was the green shirt that Steve had seen in the store the week before.

6. a. Karen had a talk with Steve.

   b. Karen had the talk with Steve.

   c. Karen talked with Steve about something.

   d. Karen had planned to talk with Steve about something, and she finally did.

7. a. Karen and Steve have an argument about once a month.

   b. Karen and Steve have the argument about once a month.

   c. They always argue about the same thing.

   d. They argue about different things.

8. a. Karen and Steve met at the movie theater.

   b. Karen and Steve met at a movie theater.

   c. There is only one movie theater in town.

   d. There are several movie theaters.

3 *Read the sentences in Exercise 2 with a partner. Student A reads either sentence **a** or sentence **b**. Student B listens and chooses the correct meaning, **c** or **d**. Then switch roles and repeat.*

D SPEAKING TOPIC

Many classes require students to participate in group discussion. One student presents information to the class and leads a discussion among the other students.

CHOOSING A TOPIC

Work in groups of four or five. Choose a topic to present to your group members. Each student should choose a different topic.

Suggested Topics

1. During the past 50 years, the divorce rate has increased in countries all over the world. What are the reasons for the increase? What are the effects of more divorces? How can divorces be prevented?

2. The word "family" has come to include a great variety of lifestyles: traditional nuclear and extended families, unmarried couples, single-parent families, "blended" families, and so on. What are the effects of having these different types of families?

3. Some people argue that unmarried couples should have the same rights as married couples. Others argue that only married people should have these rights. What are the arguments for and against each point of view?

4. There are many ways that people meet each other and decide to marry. What are some of the different ways? What are the advantages and disadvantages of each?

5. With increased travel and immigration around the world, there are more intercultural marriages taking place. What are the advantages and disadvantages of marrying someone from another country or cultural background?

PREPARING

Write an outline of your presentation following the steps below. Use the sample outline on page 180 as an example.

Step 1: Introduction—Introduce your topic. Explain any important words or ideas (see Unit 8, Section 4B).

Step 2: Body—Present different aspects or opinions about the topic. Use facts and examples from your own experience or from people you have heard about (see Unit 9, Section 4B).

Step 3: Conclusion—Give your own opinion about the topic (see Unit 3, Section 4B). List possible questions about your topic for your group discussion. Try to ask open questions (*wh-* questions) rather than *yes/no* questions (see Unit 7, Section 4C).

PRESENTING

Lead a six- to ten-minute discussion of your topic with the group.

- Ask questions from your outline for people to discuss.
- Don't talk a lot yourself; try to get the other people in your group to talk.
- Make sure each person has a chance to speak (see Unit 5, Section 4B).
- Remember that you can interrupt politely using language and gestures (see Unit 10, Section 4B).

Sample Outline

Introduction

1. Topic: Prenuptial Agreements

2. Prenuptial = before marriage

3. Prenuptial agreement = a contract between two people who are going to be married.

Body

1. Types of prenuptial agreements:

       protect money, property

       protect children

       give rules for the marriage

2. Used by:

       wealthy people (for example, movie stars)

       people starting a second marriage

3. Opinions about prenuptial agreements:

       Unromantic. You need to trust the other person. Don't think about divorce when you are getting married.

       Sensible. Many marriages end in divorce. You need to protect your money.

Conclusion

1. My opinion . . .

2. Discussion questions:

       Who should have prenuptial agreements?

       Would you ever sign a prenuptial agreement? Why or why not?

       How much legal meaning do they have?

E RESEARCH TOPICS

ORAL HISTORY

Step 1: Interview a married couple. Ask them to tell the story of how they met. Take notes during the interview. Here are some questions to help you get the conversation going:

- How did you meet? Where was it? What did you think of each other?

- How did this first meeting lead to marriage?

- When were you married?

Step 2: Make a tape recording about the story. Speak for three minutes. Don't write out the story ahead of time. Use your notes and speak clearly and naturally.

RESEARCH AND DISCUSSION

Step 1: Look up one of the following marriage topics in an encyclopedia or on the Internet.

Marriage Topics

annulment	domestic partnership	same-sex marriage
civil ceremony	no-fault divorce	(your choice)
covenant marriage	polygamy	

Use these questions to help you with your research:

- What is _____ ?

- In what cultures might you find _____ ?

- Would _____ be acceptable in your culture? Why or why not?

- What do you think about _____ ?

- Why do you feel this way?

Step 2: Meet in small groups with students who chose a different topic from you. Present your research and lead a discussion. Follow the instructions for leading a discussion (see Unit 5, Section 4B). Use facts and examples from your research in your presentation.

For Unit 10 Internet activities, visit the NorthStar Companion Website at http://www.longman.com/northstar.

Student Activities

4C. Exercise 3, page 124

Student B

*Read the following biography of comedian Jerry Seinfeld. Then write **wh-** questions to find out the missing information from your partner. Ask your partner the questions and fill in the information. Then answer your partner's questions.*

(1) _____ was born on April 29, 1954, in the city of (2) _____. He grew up in Brooklyn, and after high school he studied at Queens College.

One of Jerry's earliest jobs was to call people over the phone to sell them (3) _____. When people sent in money, Jerry's boss kept it but didn't send any bulbs. In another job, Jerry sold cheap jewelry on the street and pretended that it was expensive.

This dark period in Jerry's life did not last long. (4) _____ _____, which is how he became a star himself. Later, he was invited to perform on two famous late-night talk shows because he was so popular. And before long he had his own TV show, called (5) _____. The show was so successful that it won an Emmy award in 1993 for Best Comedy Show. Since then he has won many other awards.

Jerry does not smoke or drink. He is married to Jessica Sklar, who works as a public relations executive. They have a (6) _____ named Sascha. Today, Jerry feels that life is just about perfect!

Questions

1. *Who was born on April 29, 1954?* _____
2. _____
3. _____
4. _____
5. _____
6. _____

4D. Speaking Topic Activity, page 125

Jokes

Group 1

Q: How many archeologists does it take to change a light bulb?

A: Three. One to change it and the other two to argue about the age of the old bulb.

Q: How many managers does it take to change a light bulb?

A: Two. One to get the bulb and one to call someone to change it.

Group 2

Q: How many news reporters does it take to change a light bulb?

A: Only one, but he'll tell everyone about it.

Q: How many graduate students does it take to screw in a light bulb?

A: Only one, but it will take her up to five years to get it done.

Group 3

Q: Why did the monster eat a light bulb?

A: Because he needed a light snack.

Q: What did two penguins say when they met in the desert?

A: Long time no sea. (see)

Group 4

Q: Why was 6 afraid of 7?

A: Because 7, 8, 9. (7 ate 9)

Q: What did Mrs. Claus say to Santa as she looked out the window?

A: Looks like rain, dear. (reindeer)

Group 5

Q: What happens when you tell a duck a joke?

A: It quacks up. (cracks up)

Q: What do you call a song sung in a car?

A: A cartoon. (car-tune)

Group 6

Q: What goes up and down but doesn't move?

A: A staircase.

Q: Which two words have the most letters?

A: Post office.

Group 7

Q: What's worse than finding a worm in your apple?

A: Finding half a worm.

Q: What belongs to you but is used more by others?

A: Your name.

Group 8

Q: What gets wetter as it dries?

A: A towel.

Q: Where does Friday come before Thursday?

A: In the dictionary.

Group 9

Q: What time is it when an elephant sits on your fence?

A: Time to get a new fence.

Q: What's gray and green, gray and green, gray and green?

A: An elephant rolling down a hill with a leaf in its trunk.

Group 10

Q: How does an elephant get up a tree?

A: He sits on a seed and waits for it to grow.

Q: Why did the elephant paint his toenails red?

A: So he could hide in the strawberry field.

UNIT 9:   To Spank or Not to Spank?

1C. Exercise 1, page 146

1. c   3. b

2. c   4. a

Grammar Book References

NorthStar: Listening and Speaking, Intermediate, Second Edition	Focus on Grammar: An Intermediate Course for Reference and Practice, Second Edition	Azar's Fundamentals of English Grammar, Third Edition
Unit 1 Imperatives	**Unit 2** Imperative	**Chapter 7** Modal Auxiliaries: 7-12
Unit 2 Modals of Preference	**Unit 32** Preferences	**Chapter 7** Modal Auxiliaries: 7-14
Unit 3 Equatives and Comparatives	**Unit 23** Adjectives: Comparatives and Equatives	**Chapter 9** Comparisons
Unit 4 Infinitives of Purpose	**Unit 29** Infinitives of Purpose	**Chapter 13** Gerunds and Infinitives: 13-9
Unit 5 Modals of Ability and Possibility	**Unit 11** Ability: *Can, Could, Be able to*	**Chapter 7** Modal Auxiliaries: 7-2, 7-4
Unit 6 Simple Past Tense	**Unit 3** Simple Past Tense and **Appendix 1** Irregular Verbs	**Chapter 2** Past Time
Unit 7 *Wh-* Questions	**Unit 8** *Wh-* Questions: Subject and Predicate	**Chapter 5** Asking Questions
Unit 8 *Used to*	**Unit 4** *Used to*	**Chapter 2** Past Time: 2-11

NorthStar: Listening and Speaking, Intermediate, Second Edition	Focus on Grammar: An Intermediate Course for Reference and Practice, Second Edition	Azar's Fundamentals of English Grammar, Third Edition
Unit 9 Present Perfect	**Part IV** Present Perfect	**Chapter 4** The Present Perfect and Past Perfect: 4-2, 4-4
Unit 10 Articles	**Unit 38** Articles: Indefinite and Definite	**Chapter 11** Count/Noncount Nouns and Articles: 11-1, 11-8

Audioscript

UNIT 1: Advertising on the Air

A. LISTENING ONE: *Advertising on the Air*

Professor: Good morning, everyone!

Good morning. As you remember, last week we talked about the history of radio advertising. And so today we're going to continue by talking about techniques that advertisers use to get us to buy the products they're selling. In other words . . . the methods they use to persuade us to buy. One of the most effective techniques is to manipulate, or control, our emotions. Advertisers call this an emotional appeal. Today I'm going to talk about several emotional appeals. And to show you . . . to show you what I'm talking about, I'm going to play some real radio ads. Is everyone with me at this point? O.K., then. Let's get started.

LISTENING FOR MAIN IDEAS

Exercise 1

Professor: Good morning, everyone!

Good morning. As you remember, last week we talked about the history of radio advertising. And so today we're going to continue by talking about techniques that advertisers use to get us to buy the products they're selling. In other words . . . the methods they use to persuade us to buy. One of the most effective techniques is to manipulate, or control, our emotions. Advertisers call this an emotional appeal. Today I'm going to talk about several emotional appeals. And to show you . . . to show you what I'm talking about, I'm going to play some real radio ads. Is everyone with me at this point? O.K., then. Let's get started.

One of the most popular emotional appeals is the appeal to humor. If something is funny it's likely to grab us . . . our attention I mean. So, funny ads are often easy to remember. They also give us a good feeling . . . which is another reason why humor is popular. Here's an example of a humorous ad:

Speaker: It's flea season again! Fleas! Those pesky bugs jump into your dog's hair, bite his skin, make him itch. Unfortunately, most flea treatments involve bathing with harsh chemicals. Not fun for me—or my dog. That's why I'm getting the Doggie's Friend flea collar. It goes around your dog's neck and makes a noise that drives fleas crazy. . . . So off they jump!

Announcer: Don't delay. Get a Doggie's Friend today.

Professor: Well . . . obviously the man's very happy with his Doggie's Friend collar. Notice the doggie noises in the background. They're cute and funny, which helps us remember the ad. Even the name—Doggie's Friend—is cute . . . so the humor . . . well . . . it seems to fit the product. This is important . . . fitting the right appeal with the right product. It wouldn't work to use a funny ad for a serious product . . . say . . . say to advertise a law firm that specializes in divorce. That wouldn't fit.

All right, now let's examine another appeal. The next kind of ad appeals to our egos. The appeal to ego . . . yes . . . you have a question, Jake?

Jake: I'm sorry, what do you mean by ego?

Professor: What do I mean by ego? Well . . . our egos make us do things to look good in front of others. For example, we might buy . . . say, a luxury car to look rich, or . . . join a health club to get in shape . . . all because we want to look good. Does that make sense? Good! So here's an ad that appeals to ego.

Liz: Hi, Kathy! . . . Say . . . did you do something to your hair?

Kathy: Yup! I colored it with Younger You.

Liz: It's amazing! You really do look younger!

Kathy: Thanks! Now, people don't believe I'm a grandmother.

Liz: I should try it.

Kathy: It's so easy to use. Just mix it with your shampoo, wash, and rinse.

Liz: Sounds great!

Announcer: Only five minutes to a younger you.

Professor: O.K. So how does this product make you look better? . . . Yes, Linda . . .

Linda: It colors gray hair?

Professor: Right! Notice the use of the admiring friend who tells Kathy how great she looks. That's the appeal to ego. O.K., any questions before we move on to the next appeal?

LISTENING FOR DETAILS

(Repeat Listening for Main Ideas)

REACTING TO THE LISTENING

Exercise 1

Doggie's Friend Ad

Speaker: It's flea season again! Fleas! Those pesky bugs jump into your dog's hair, bite his skin, make him itch. Unfortunately, most flea treatments involve bathing with harsh chemicals. Not fun for me—or my dog. That's why I'm getting the Doggie's Friend flea collar. It goes around your dog's neck and makes a noise that drives fleas crazy. . . . So off they jump!

Announcer: Don't delay. Get a Doggie's Friend today.

Younger You Ad

Liz: Hi, Kathy! . . . Say . . . did you do something to your hair?

Kathy: Yup! I colored it with Younger You.

Liz: It's amazing! You really do look younger!

Kathy: Thanks! Now, people don't believe I'm a grandmother.

Liz: I should try it.

Kathy: It's so easy to use. Just mix it with your shampoo, wash, and rinse.

Liz: Sounds great!

Announcer: Only five minutes to a younger you.

B. LISTENING TWO: *Negative Appeals*

Thief Buster Ad

Speaker: You park your car, and your worst nightmare happens! When you come back . . . it's gone! It can happen anywhere . . . and chances are, one day, it will happen to you!

189

That's why you need the incredible Thief Buster security system. It's easy to use and 100 percent effective. If someone so much as touches your car, an alarm will ring. And if that doesn't stop the thief, the engine will automatically turn off when he starts the car. So why put your car at risk any longer? Get a Thief Buster security system today! Thief Buster . . . protection for your peace of mind!

Rinse Away Ad

Brad: Hello?

Lisa: Hi, Brad! It's Lisa. How was your job interview?

Brad: It was terrible! I was wearing that dark blue jacket . . . you know . . . the one with the gold buttons. . . .

Lisa: Uh-huh?

Brad: Well, I noticed that the boss kept looking at my shoulders. I couldn't figure it out, so I took a quick look and saw all these white, powdery flakes.

Lisa: From your head?

Brad: Yeah, it was dandruff! You could really see it too . . . because of the jacket. It was so embarrassing . . . and it totally threw me off. I just couldn't concentrate on the questions.

Announcer: Dandruff can be a small problem with big consequences. Luckily there's Rinse Away dandruff shampoo to take care of even your toughest dandruff. Don't let the embarrassment of an itchy, flaky scalp slow you down. Just Rinse Away and feel the confidence. Rinse Away—your sure cure for dandruff!

A. PRONUNCIATION: *Highlighting*

Liz: It's amazing! You really do look younger!

Kathy: Thanks! Now, people don't believe I'm a grandmother.

Liz: I should try it.

Exercise 1

1. **Kathy:** Hello?

   Liz: Kathy! I took your advice!

   Kathy: What advice?

   Liz: I colored my hair.

   Kathy: With Younger You?

   Liz: Yes! It's great!

2. **Kathy:** Did you hear about that new flea collar?

   Liz: Yes, I'm going to the pet store today. How about you?

   Kathy: I think I'll stop by tomorrow.

UNIT 2: Pushing the Limit

LISTENING ONE: *Journal of a Mountain Climber*

Jennifer: Face diagonally. Plant your ice axe in front. Plant your left foot. Plant your right. Axe, left, right, pause. Axe, left, right, pause.

LISTENING FOR MAIN IDEAS

Jennifer: We're at Helen Lake . . . at 10,400 feet . . . It's 5 A.M. It's still dark, but I can see 'cause the moon's really bright. I'm excited. This has been a personal goal for five years, and here I

am . . . about to start the final ascent. . . . But getting started's always hard. My body hurts from yesterday's climb. Better go. Tom, Doug, and Dave are ready and waiting for me.

Avalanche Gulch . . . 11,000 feet . . . 6 A.M. There's a rhythm . . . to this climbing. Face diagonally. Plant your ice axe in front. Plant your left foot. Plant your right. Axe, left, right, pause, axe, left, right, pause. . . . The rhythm . . . helps me keep going. . . . I'm not thinking . . . about the top of the mountain . . . only the next three steps.

Oh my gosh, that was close. It's 8 A.M. now. I was coming up an icy ridge, at the Red Banks . . . about 12,000 feet, and I slipped. I started sliding down the mountain. For a few seconds, I was so terrified, I really thought I was going to go spinning out of control. But I dug my axe into the snow, and stopped myself. What a rush! I can't believe I did that! I feel so alive!

It's really windy. I guess that's why they call this Misery Hill. It just blows right through you. I'm cold. Got to keep my head down and keep pushing. This hill is deceiving. Just as you reach the top of a ridge, you see another one ahead. I'm thinking about life on the ground. A few days ago I was worrying about, Will I be late for work? What should I make for dinner? That seems so, so unimportant now. Here . . . here it's a fight against nature . . . against yourself. Every part of you is pushed to the limit.

Oh my gosh! There's the summit. I'm at 13,600 feet and it's 10 A.M. I can see it . . . like . . . like a shining jewel at the end of that flat ridge. My heart's pumping. I have the sensation that . . . that my body's floating. I'm not tired now. Just going to cross this ridge . . . snowy mountains on either side. There's Dave and Tom a bit ahead. Doug's just behind. We're going to make it! I'm so excited!

Doug and I are climbing up the last section . . . round this rock . . . and . . . we're here!. . . at the summit! . . . 14,000 . . . 162 feet at . . . 10:45 A.M.!

Tom: *(singing)* Climb every mountain . . . la la la la . . .

Jennifer: Tom's singing to us as we stumble in.

Doug: You made it! Congratulations.

Dave: I wasn't sure if I was going to make that last part.

Doug: Yeah. That wind was rough. Did you sign the book?

Dave: Where is it?

Jennifer: The sun is almost directly ahead. What a view! Mountains upon mountains as far as the eye can see . . . a little lake, about the size of a postcard from here . . . the town of Shasta way in the distance. There's a small plane flying below me. Some soft clouds drift by . . . below me. Everything is below me. Woo hoo! I made it to the summit!

LISTENING FOR DETAILS

(Repeat Listening for Main Ideas)

REACTING TO THE LISTENING

Exercise 1

Excerpt 1

Jennifer: For a few seconds, I was so terrified, I really thought I was going to go spinning out of control. But I dug my axe into the snow, and stopped myself. What a rush! I can't believe I did that! I feel so alive!

Excerpt 2

Jennifer: It's really windy. I guess that's why they call this Misery Hill. It just blows right through you. I'm cold. Got to keep my head down and keep pushing. This hill is deceiving. Just as you reach the top of a ridge, you see another one ahead.

Excerpt 3

Jennifer: The sun is almost directly ahead. What a view! Mountains upon mountains as far as the eye can see . . . a little lake, about the size of a postcard from here . . . the town of Shasta way in the distance. There's a small plane flying below me. Some soft clouds drift by . . . below me. Everything is below me. Woo hoo! I made it to the summit!

LISTENING TWO: *Sensation Seekers*

Professor: So, we've already talked a bit about the growth of extreme sports—things like mountain climbing and parachuting. As psychologists, we need to ask ourselves, why is this person doing this? Why do people take these risks and put themselves in danger when they don't have to?

One common trait among risk takers is that they enjoy strong feelings or sensations. We call this trait "sensation seeking." A "sensation seeker" is someone who's always looking for new sensations. What else do we know about sensation seekers?

Well, as I said, sensation seekers like strong emotion. You can see this trait in many parts of a person's life, not just in extreme sports. For example, many sensation seekers enjoy hard rock music. They like the loud sound and strong emotion of the songs. Similarly, sensation seekers enjoy frightening horror movies. They like the feeling of being scared and horrified while watching the movie. This feeling is even stronger for extreme sports, where the person faces real danger. Sensation seekers feel that danger is very exciting.

In addition, sensation seekers like new experiences that force them to push their personal limits. For them, repeating the same things every day is boring. Many sensation seekers choose jobs that include risk, such as starting a new business or being an emergency room doctor. These jobs are different every day, so they never know what will happen. That's why many sensation seekers also like extreme sports. When you climb a mountain or jump out of an airplane, you never know what will happen. The activity is always new and different.

PRONUNCIATION: *Front Vowels*

reach   rich

pain   pen

Exercise 1

1. reach	rich	6. main	men
2. pain	pen	7. fail	fell
3. miss	mess	8. pit	pet
4. sit	set	9. seat	sit
5. reason	risen	10. seek	sick

Exercise 2

1. reach	6. men
2. pen	7. fail
3. mess	8. pet
4. sit	9. seat
5. reason	10. sick

Exercise 4

1. a deep breath	6. a little rest
2. keep the rhythm	7. sensation seekers
3. risk takers	8. a steep hill
4. windy weather	9. the thrill of danger
5. a steep ascent	10. my favorite people

UNIT 3: Too Good to Be True

A. LISTENING ONE: *Too Good to Be True*

Reporter: Every day, innocent people are victims, losing money to telephone con artists who'll tell you anything to get your money. In the United States alone, people lose about 40 billion dollars each year through telephone fraud. I'm Nadine Chow. Today we're going to listen to a real phone call to learn what these con artists say in order to swindle people, and what you can do to protect yourself.

Frank: Good afternoon, is Ms. Suzanne Markham in?

Suzanne: Yes, that's me.

Frank: Suzanne, this is Frank Richland from Sunshine Vacations. How are you doing today?

Suzanne: I'm fine.

Frank: Ma'am, are you ready for a big surprise?

LISTENING FOR MAIN IDEAS

Reporter: Every day, innocent people are victims, losing money to telephone con artists who'll tell you anything to get your money. In the United States alone, people lose about 40 billion dollars each year through telephone fraud. I'm Nadine Chow. Today we're going to listen to a real phone call to learn what these con artists say in order to swindle people, and what you can do to protect yourself.

Frank: Good afternoon, is Ms. Suzanne Markham in?

Suzanne: Yes, that's me.

Frank: Suzanne, this is Frank Richland from Sunshine Vacations. How are you doing today?

Suzanne: I'm fine.

Frank: Ma'am, are you ready for a big surprise? Because I have some great news! It's my pleasure to tell you that you've just won our Grand Prize!

Suzanne: The Grand Prize? Really? What did I win?

Frank: You've done it! You're our lucky winner! You've just won a luxury vacation to Hawaii—eight days and seven nights in beautiful Waikiki! Your meals, airfare, and hotel costs are all included! You pay nothing! Congratulations!

Suzanne: Oh, my gosh! I don't believe it! Really? I can't believe it!

Reporter: Sounds great, doesn't it? Almost too good to be true. Frank Richland is a telephone con artist. He's using one of the most common scams in the book—telling the victim she has just won a big prize. The problem is, there isn't any prize. However, to make the prize seem real, the con artist talks about what will happen next.

Frank: As soon as we finish the paperwork, I'm going to mail the ticket to your house. Then you can use it for a vacation any time in the next year. I also have to get a picture of you to put on the cover of our national magazine. . . . We want to show all our customers the lucky lady who won our Grand Prize!

Suzanne: Oh, wow! This is great! I've always wanted to go to Hawaii!! My husband will be so happy!

Reporter: The con artist has done the first half of his job. Suzanne is excited about winning a prize. But now he tells her what she has to do to get it.

Frank: Now, before I send out the prize, we need to complete some paperwork. You see, I have to give someone this prize today. I want to give it to you. But to hold the prize, you need to send a small deposit. Then we can send you your prize.

Suzanne: How much is the deposit?

Frank: It's just $500.

Suzanne: Mmmm . . . $500 . . . That's a lot of money.

Reporter: Now that the victim knows that she has to send money, she's not sure if she can trust Frank. To get the money, the con artist has to reassure her that he is telling the truth.

Frank: Suzanne, to tell you the truth, I get the feeling that you don't trust me. But really, I'm trying to get this vacation for you. I'd like to send it to you right now, with no deposit, but I have to follow the rules. I need to get that deposit from you. I know that you're really going to enjoy this vacation, so I really want to give it to you.

Suzanne: Well, it does sound wonderful!

Reporter: After he feels that the victim trusts him, the con artist puts pressure on the victim to make a quick decision.

Frank: The thing is, you have to take the vacation now. I can only wait 24 hours, and then I've gotta give it to someone else. So you really need to send me the five hundred dollars today.

Suzanne: Uh-huh.

Frank: So, to make sure I understand, you're going to send me five hundred dollars today so I can send you your prize, right? You've got to do it right away.

Suzanne: O.K. . . . Who do I send the money to?

Frank: That's Sunshine Vacations. 703 Western Avenue . . .

Reporter: And there you have it. Suzanne sent the money and—you guessed it—she never heard from Sunshine Vacations again. You might think that Suzanne is more gullible than most, but the truth is, anyone can be a victim of fraud. So be careful. Don't get swindled. Remember—if something seems too good to be true, it probably is!

LISTENING FOR DETAILS

(Repeat Listening for Main Ideas)

REACTING TO THE LISTENING

Exercise 1

Excerpt 1

Frank: This is Frank Richland from Sunshine Vacations. . . . Ma'am, are you ready for a big surprise? Because I have some great news! It's my pleasure to tell you that you've just won our Grand Prize!

Suzanne: The Grand Prize? Really? What did I win?

Excerpt 2

Frank: As soon as we finish the paperwork, I'm going to mail the ticket to your house. Then you can use it for a vacation anytime in the next year. I also have to get a picture of you to put on the cover of our national magazine. . . . We want to show all our customers the lucky lady who won our Grand Prize!

Suzanne: Oh, wow! This is great! I've always wanted to go to Hawaii!! My husband will be so happy!

Excerpt 3

Frank: Now, before I send out the prize, we need to complete some paperwork. You see, I have to give someone this prize today. I want to give it to you. But to hold the prize, you need to send a small deposit. Then we can send you your prize.

Suzanne: How much is the deposit?

Excerpt 4

Frank: So, to make sure I understand, you're going to send me $500 today so I can send you your prize, right? You've got to do it right away.

Suzanne: O.K. . . . Who do I send the money to?

B. LISTENING TWO: *Interviews*

Victim 1

Joe L.: I don't really know why I sent him the money. My daughter's always telling me not to give out my credit card number over the phone, but this guy Frank was so nice and friendly that I believed him. I guess I'm pretty gullible. If someone tells me something, I usually believe them. That's O.K. most of the time, but sometimes it gets me into trouble.

Victim 2

Rosa A.: Frank seemed like such a nice young man, and so concerned about me. You see, I lost my husband a year ago, and I don't have many friends. I don't get many phone calls and I sometimes get very lonely, so I really enjoyed talking to him. I really thought I could trust him.

Victim 3

Peter S.: I've heard about telephone fraud like this, and I always thought I was very careful. But while I was talking to Frank, I kept thinking about how much my wife would like going to Hawaii. I lost my job recently, so I don't have any extra money. I guess I got too excited about the free vacation and didn't think carefully.

Victim 4

Beth G.: Well, Frank put so much pressure on me! He kept saying that he wanted to help me, and how I had to decide right away. He said that if I didn't send the money, he'd give the prize to someone else. I wasn't sure I could trust him, but he made me decide so quickly; I just didn't have time to think!

A. PRONUNCIATION: *Reductions*

Exercise 1

Frank:	Do you wanna get a prize?
	Do you wanna get a prize?
Suzanne:	Yes, I wanna get a prize.
	Yes, I wanna get a prize.
Frank:	First you hafta send the money.
	First you hafta send the money.
Suzanne:	I don't wanna send the money.
	I don't wanna send the money.

Frank: You hafta send it now.
            You hafta send it now.
Suzanne: I'm gonna call the cops.
            I'm gonna call the cops.

UNIT 4: The Art of Storytelling

A. LISTENING ONE: "Lavender"

Robert and David were good friends. Late one spring evening, they were driving to a spring social. As they drove along the road, Robert and David both realized that they didn't have dates! So David said to Robert, "Some good friend you are. What happened to our dates for the evening?"

"Oh, I'm sorry. I just couldn't get them to go."

"Well, we'll find dates at the dance. There'll be lots of girls there without partners."

As they drove along the road, the headlights fell on someone walking along the side of the highway.

LISTENING FOR MAIN IDEAS

Robert and David were good friends. Late one spring evening, they were driving to a spring social. As they drove along the road, Robert and David both realized that they didn't have dates! So David said to Robert, "Some good friend you are. What happened to our dates for the evening?"

"Oh, I'm sorry. I just couldn't get them to go."

"Well, we'll find dates at the dance. There'll be lots of girls there without partners."

As they drove along the road, the headlights fell on someone walking along the side of the highway. As they approached the person walking, they could see that it was a young girl, dressed in a lavender evening dress. Robert looked at David, David looked at Robert, and they both smiled. They slowed the car down, and when they stopped, they said to the young woman, "We're on our way to the social."

"Oh," she said, "so am I!"

"Would you like to ride?"

"I would indeed," she said.

She got into the back of the car. Robert and David introduced themselves and she said, "I'm Lavender, just like my dress. Just call me Lavender."

As they drove along, they decided that they would be together that night. At the dance, Robert danced with Lavender, David danced with Lavender, and as the evening wore on, the spring air turned a little cool. And Robert said to Lavender, "Are you cold? Would you like my coat?"

"Oh, yes," she said, "I am just a bit chilled."

And Robert said, "I think it's raining outside. Could we drive you home?"

"Oh, yes," she said, "Thank you. I didn't want to walk on the highway alone tonight."

And as they started down the highway, Lavender explained that both her mom and dad were just a little strict. And it would be very difficult to explain how she had come home with two strange young men. So it would be easier to stop at the edge of the driveway and she could walk to the house without any explanation to her parents. And Robert and David understood. And as they stopped at the edge of the driveway, Lavender got out, blew them a kiss from the tip of her fingers, and walked down the driveway and through the trees toward the house. And then they realized that she still had the coat!

David said, "Tomorrow. We'll get it back tomorrow. That will be the excuse we use to come and visit."

Early the next morning, David and Robert were on the highway, driving toward the house. But as they drove up and down the highway, they couldn't seem to find the driveway.

"It was here!"

"No, it was over there!"

"It was here," said Robert, "but look, it's all grown up. There're weeds, and grass, and rocks. It wasn't grown up last night! But this is the driveway . . . you see, there's a house between the trees."

So they stopped the car and got out, and walked along the driveway. And as they cleared the trees, they could see the house. And Robert said to David, "Are you sure that we're in the right place? Look at this house. Look at the windows— they're all broken! And look how the door hangs from the hinges! This couldn't be the place!" They walked to the back of the house. And there, in a little picket fence, was a little family cemetery with five, six, seven gravestones. And hanging on one of the gravestones, a middle-sized gravestone, was the coat. And as they lifted the coat from the stone they both said, "Aaah!"

The name on the gravestone was "Lavender." They had spent the evening with a ghost. And that's the end of that!

LISTENING FOR DETAILS

(Repeat Listening for Main Ideas)

REACTING TO THE LISTENING

Exercise 1

Excerpt 1

. . . And Robert said to Lavender, "Are you cold? Would you like my coat?"

"Oh, yes," she said, "I am just a bit chilled."

And Robert said, "I think it's raining outside. Could we drive you home?"

"Oh, yes," she said, "Thank you. I didn't want to walk on the highway alone tonight."

Excerpt 2

. . . But as they drove up and down the highway, they couldn't seem to find the driveway.

"It was here!"

"No, it was over there!"

"It was here," said Robert, "but look, it's all grown up. There're weeds, and grass, and rocks. It wasn't grown up last night! But this is the driveway . . . you see, there's a house between the trees."

Excerpt 3

. . . They walked to the back of the house. And there, in a little picket fence, was a little family cemetery with five, six, seven gravestones. And hanging on one of the gravestones, a middle-sized gravestone, was the coat. And as they lifted the coat from the stone they both said, "Aaah!"

The name on the gravestone was "Lavender."

B. LISTENING TWO: *An Interview with Jackie Torrence*

Exercise 1

Interviewer: You have an interesting technique that you recommend for storytelling, for learning a story. And that is to read it five times before you tell it. Why is that?

Torrence: Yes. Well, the first time you tell a story, you see that you like it. And I always say don't ever tell a story you don't like, 'cause you've wasted your time and the time of your listener.

Then, the second time you read, read it for the pictures. Read it for the pictures that you're going to create. As you read about the characters, you read a personality into those characters. You give those characters a look, you see them as familiar individuals. They may look like your husband, your wife, your daughter, your son.

The third time you read it, read it for the words. Now this is a very important part of the story because words make that story. You can make it or break it by saying the right or wrong words.

A. PRONUNCIATION: *Rhythm of Prepositional Phrases*

Exercise 1

1. Robert and David drove from their house.

2. Lavender was waiting on the road.

3. She walked with Robert.

4. The three friends went to the dance.

5. They got back in the car.

6. Robert and David were looking at the coat in the backyard.

7. Robert pointed to the gravestone.

8. They ran for the car.

Exercise 2

1. come to dinner	come tomorrow
2. Thanks for getting a job.	Hank's forgetting his job.
3. It's hard to dance.	It's cold today.
4. a fortune at school	a fortunate school
5. at nine	arrive
6. point at Tom	pointed top

UNIT 5: Separated by the Same Language

A. LISTENING ONE: *Accent and Identity*

Peter: Also, whenever I opened my mouth I could see people thinking, "I wonder where he's from," and that would be the first question: "Where are you from?" And then I'd have to go into this long explanation about my background. I guess I got tired of it.

LISTENING FOR MAIN IDEAS

Lisa: Hi. This is Lisa. I'm doing a project on accents for my sociolinguistics course, so I'm interviewing some of my friends from grad school.

Lisa: This is my friend Peter. Peter, can you give me a little background on where you grew up?

Peter: St. Lucia, in the West Indies, is what I call home. And I've lived in the States, here in North Carolina, for six years.

Lisa: So do you feel that you have an accent?

Peter: Well, I wasn't aware of my accent until I came here. Obviously, growing up in St. Lucia, no one told me I had an accent because we all spoke the same way.

Lisa: So how did you feel about your accent when you came here?

Peter: Well, when I came here, many people commented on my accent. So I started to be aware of it. I still get comments all the time. I mean they always say things, things that . . .

Lisa: Like?

Peter: Oh, just, I mean, people say, "Oh, I love your accent. It's so musical."

Lisa: So they like your accent.

Peter: Yes, but I also remember—when I first came—I felt that I spoke so slowly, everyone else spoke much faster. . . . Some people stereotyped me because of that. I could tell that they were thinking, "He's not very bright." You know, "A slow mouth has a slow brain . . . he speaks slowly so he must be thinking slowly, too." So that made me feel pretty self-conscious. Also, whenever I opened my mouth I could see people thinking, "I wonder where he's from," and that would be the first question: "Where are you from?" And then I'd have to go into this long explanation about my background. I guess I got tired of it.

Lisa: But wasn't that a good way to meet people?

Peter: Hmm. Maybe. . . . But there's a difference between meeting people and making friends. I mean . . . here I was, a first-year student, meeting lots of people, but I always felt that the other students didn't really understand who I was. It made me feel like . . . like I didn't fit in.

Lisa: So did you try to fit in?

Peter: Yeah, I did. Not intentionally. Funny how that happens, but I'd hear myself saying "class" instead of "class." And "water" instead of "water." And I'd try to speak quickly. Oh . . . and I'd try to use the slang that everyone else used. A lot of the slang was different. . . .

Lisa: But . . . but you don't have an American accent now. What happened?

Peter: Well, I started to feel differently when I moved to International House.

Lisa: International House?

Peter: Yes, this house on campus where foreign students lived, and Americans who were interested in foreign students. I started going to parties there and really felt like I fit in because everyone had a different accent. They didn't stereotype me, and everyone accepted everyone else's accent. Hmm . . . I guess that's the main thing. When people accept you, then you can speak the way you want.

Lisa: So it sounds like you want to keep your accent.

Peter: I do now. It's part of who I am . . . part of my identity. But of course I'm also older now. I'm not trying to fit in with a crowd, so I'm comfortable with the way I speak.

LISTENING FOR DETAILS

(Repeat Listening for Main Ideas)

REACTING TO THE LISTENING

Exercise 1

Excerpt 1

Peter: Well, I wasn't aware of my accent until I came here. Obviously, growing up in St. Lucia, no one told me I had an accent because we all spoke the same way.

Excerpt 2

Peter: Yes, but I also remember—when I first came—I felt that I spoke so slowly, everyone else spoke much faster. . . . Some people stereotyped me because of that. I could tell that they were thinking, "He's not very bright." You know, "A slow mouth has a slow brain . . . he speaks slowly so he must be thinking slowly, too." So that made me feel pretty self-conscious.

Excerpt 3

Peter: Yes, this house on campus where foreign students lived, and Americans who were interested in foreign students. I started going to parties there and really felt like I fit in because everyone had a different accent. They didn't stereotype me, and everyone accepted everyone else's accent. Hmm . . . I guess that's the main thing. When people accept you, then you can speak the way you want.

B. LISTENING TWO: *Code Switching*

Professor: Today I want to talk about "code switching." Code switching is when a person switches, or changes, from one way of talking to another. Usually, it happens in different situations. So, a person may use one dialect at home, and then code switch to another dialect at school or work.

One example of code switching is the way teenagers change their speech when talking to their friends or to an adult. You probably experienced this as a teenager—there were some slang words that you used only with your friends, not with parents or teachers. And your parents probably hated the way you spoke, right? Parents always hate teen slang. But anyway, this slang, it's really a teenage dialect. And when teens switch from the teen dialect to the standard dialect, this is code switching.

Let me give you an example. Let's say a teenager says to his friend, "Gotta bounce. Me 'n' the crew're goin' shoppin' for some phat gear."

Did you understand that? Let me translate: "Gotta bounce" means "I've gotta leave"; "the crew" means "my friends"; "phat gear" means "nice clothes." So the teen's basically saying that he's going shopping with friends.

Why do teenagers use this dialect? Well, because it's an important way for teens to show their identity—to show that they fit in with their friends. It also shows that they are separate from their parents. So by code switching into a teenage dialect with their friends, a teenager is saying, "I'm one of you."

O.K.—any questions . . . ?

A. PRONUNCIATION: *Can/Can't*

Student A: Can you speak any foreign languages?

Student B: Yes, I can. I can speak Chinese. But I can't speak very fluently yet. How about you?

Student A: I can read French, but I can't speak it very well.

Exercise 1

1. She can't take that class.
2. He can speak French.
3. I can't understand American slang.
4. We can speak that dialect.
5. I can't recognize his accent.
6. She can't fit in.
7. I can comment on that.
8. She invited me to come. I said that I can.

UNIT 6: "Culture and Commerce"

A. LISTENING ONE: *Radio News Report*

Reporter: Each year around 10,000 tourists visit three small villages along the Thai/Myanmar border to see the famous long-necked women. The attraction is a tradition that requires women to stretch their necks by wearing brass coils. Originally from the Pa Daung tribe, the women and their families have been running from Myanmar to Thailand since the 1980s to escape poverty and war. Their new lives are very different from their lives as farmers in Myanmar. Now they spend their days talking with tourists, posing for pictures, and selling handmade souvenirs.

LISTENING FOR MAIN IDEAS

Announcer: Critics call it "a human zoo." Tour companies consider it a tourist attraction. Whichever the case, the long-necked women of Pa Daung have become an important source of money for several small villages on the border of Thailand and Myanmar. Reporter Mike Danforth has this report.

Tour Leader: Welcome to Nai Soi. Please buy your ticket here.

Reporter: Each year around 10,000 tourists visit three small villages along the Thai/Myanmar border to see the famous long-necked women. The attraction is a tradition that requires women to stretch their necks by wearing brass coils. Originally from the Pa Daung tribe, the women and their families have been running from Myanmar to Thailand since the 1980s to escape poverty and war. Their new lives are very different from their lives as farmers in Myanmar. Now they spend their days talking with tourists, posing for pictures, and selling handmade souvenirs.

When a Pa Daung girl turns 5, a thick coil of brass is wrapped around her neck. At different times in her life, more coils are added until her neck carries up to 25 brass rings, weighing 11 to 22 pounds. The coils push up her chin and press down her collarbone, making her neck longer. Pa Peiy, a young woman with 20 neck rings, describes her early years of neck stretching.

Pa Peiy: At first it was painful, but now it's O.K. Now sleeping, eating, working . . . everything is O.K. But I cannot take it off . . . so this is my life.

Reporter: It truly is her life. Pa Peiy's neck is now so weak that if she takes off the coils, her head will fall forward and she will stop breathing. Despite the discomfort, Pa Daung women in Thailand continue to wear the coils even though the tradition has almost disappeared in Myanmar. Why? Because there's money in it. Ma Nang, a graceful woman with 24 neck rings explains:

Ma Nang: In Myanmar I worked hard growing food. Now I sit and tourists take pictures. In one month I get seventy to eighty dollars. It's easy, and it's good money for my family. Sometimes I'm tired of tourists always looking . . . but it's good money.

Reporter: Each year, as the long-necked women have become more and more popular, the controversy about them has increased. In a hotel near Nai Soi, tourists discuss whether or not to visit the village. Sandra, a Canadian woman, feels that it's fine to visit.

Sandra: I don't really see a problem. I mean this is their tradition . . . and so if I go, it's like I'm helping them to preserve it. Spending my money is also helping them . . . you know, to feed their families and so on. They need the tourists.

Reporter: Fredrick, from Germany, feels different.

Fredrick: Actually I don't see that we're preserving tradition at all. This tradition has died in Myanmar already. These women are just hurting their bodies to entertain us. It's like paying to go see animals in a zoo. It's degrading.

Reporter: For now, the future of the long-necked women is easy to predict. As long as there are tourists who will pay to see them, they will continue to wrap their daughters' necks. The controversy continues, with one side seeing the villages as examples of how tourism can save dying traditions, and others criticizing it as harmful and degrading to the Pa Daung women.

LISTENING FOR DETAILS

(Repeat Listening for Main Ideas)

REACTING TO THE LISTENING

Exercise 1

Excerpt 1

Pa Peiy: At first it was painful, but now it's O.K. Now sleeping, eating, working . . . everything is O.K. But I cannot take it off . . . so this is my life.

Excerpt 2

Ma Nang: In Myanmar I worked hard growing food. Now I sit and tourists take pictures. In one month I get seventy to eighty dollars. It's easy, and it's good money for my family. Sometimes I'm tired of tourists always looking . . . but it's good money.

Exercise 2

Sandra

I don't really see a problem. I mean this is their tradition . . . and so if I go it's like I'm helping them to preserve it. Spending my money is also helping them . . . you know, to feed their families and so on. They need the tourists.

Fredrick

Actually I don't see that we're preserving tradition at all. This tradition has died in Myanmar already. These women are just hurting their bodies to entertain us. It's like paying to go see animals in a zoo. It's degrading.

B. LISTENING TWO: *Town Hall Meeting in Hyannis, Cape Cod*

Mayor: O.K. Let's start with the first item on our agenda— how to deal with the problems created by too many tourists on Cape Cod during the summer. I'd like to start by identifying some of the problems.

Woman 1: Well, for one, the traffic is just terrible in the summer! In winter, it takes me about 15 minutes to drive into town. But in the summer, it can be 45 minutes or more. It's ridiculous!

Man: In my mind, the biggest problem is housing. The cost of buying or renting a home here is way too high! Pretty much, you can't afford it on a regular salary . . . all the homes are being sold to rich people for vacation homes. And that leaves nothing for the working people who live here. I mean I own a seafood restaurant, O.K.? And I've got a waitress who's living in her car right now because she can't find any other place to live. Now that's ridiculous!

Woman 2: Can I say something? O.K., I know it's difficult to have all these tourists around during the summer, but I, for one, am very happy to have them. I run a souvenir shop, and I do about 80 percent of my business for the year in the summer. And I'm not the only one. Tourists are the lifeblood of our community. We've got to keep them coming.

Mayor: O.K. . . . O.K., I'd like to hear from everyone tonight, so let's move on now. Can I ask . . .

A. PRONUNCIATION: *Past Tense Endings*

Exercise 1

1. harmed
2. allowed
3. helped
4. invited
5. improved
6. ended
7. visited
8. stretched
9. rubbed
10. wrapped
11. talked
12. attracted

Exercise 3

1. We met a long-necked woman who talked about her experience.
2. She said that when she was 5 years old, her mother wrapped a brass coil around her neck.
3. The coil stretched out her neck.
4. It was uncomfortable, but it attracted a lot of tourists.
5. The money from the tourists improved her life.
6. The woman allowed us to take photos.
7. She invited us to visit her house.
8. Our visit ended after we bought some souvenirs.

UNIT 7: Joking Around

A. LISTENING ONE: *What's So Funny?*

Host: Hi, and welcome to *Talk About It*. I'm Carmen Fiallo and today's topic is humor. Our guest is Dr. James Sanders, a sociologist who studies humor. He's just written a new book, *American Humor,* about jokes in the United States. Good morning, Dr. Sanders.

LISTENING FOR MAIN IDEAS

Host: Hi, and welcome to *Talk About It*. I'm Carmen Fiallo, and today's topic is humor. Our guest is Dr. James Sanders, a sociologist who studies humor. He's just written a new book, *American Humor,* about jokes in the United States. Good morning, Dr. Sanders.

Sanders: Hi, nice to be here.

Host: Now, I have to laugh. You study jokes? That's not really a serious area of study, is it?

Sanders: Oh, but I take my work very seriously. Actually, humor tells us a lot about society and how we think.

Host: Can you give us an example?

Sanders: Well, we often make jokes about things we're uncomfortable with. Like jokes about death or marriage problems. They help us deal with our feelings about these issues. But mostly, humor is a way for people to socialize.

Host: How so?

Sanders: People enjoy the feeling of laughter. It feels good and we like to make other people laugh. It's a way for people to connect—a way to bond with each other.

Host: So, let's do some human bonding here. Let us know— what tickles your funny bone? What makes you laugh? Give us a call with your favorite joke. . . . Hello, Andrew, you're on *Talk About It*.

Andrew: Hi. I want to tell you my favorite joke.

Host: Andrew, how old are you?

Andrew: Ummm, nine?

Host: O.K., great! What's the joke?

Andrew: Why'd the farmer put bells on his cows?

Host: I give up.

Andrew: Because their horns don't work.

Host: Great one, Andrew. Thanks for calling.

Sanders: This is a great example of one of the most common types of jokes: a pun. We love this type of joke because we love to play with words. Puns can be found in any language, and they are one of the earliest types of humor as well. We see puns in the writings of Shakespeare and in ancient writing from Greece and China.

Host: Fascinating. O.K., let's go to another call. Hi, Joan, you're on *Talk About It.*

Joan: Hi, Carmen.

Host: Do you have a joke for us?

Joan: Sure, but first, I want you to know that I'm a lawyer.

Host: So you're going to tell us a lawyer joke?

Joan: Right. Because I know, everyone loves lawyers.

Host: O.K.

Joan: O.K. . . . A man goes to see a famous lawyer. The man asks, "How much do you charge?" The lawyer answers, "I charge $200 to answer three questions." The man says, "Isn't that expensive?" "Yes, it is," replies the lawyer. "Now, what's your third question?"

Host: Thanks, Joan. . . . Lawyer jokes. Dr. Sanders, what can you tell us about them?

Sanders: Well, they belong in the category of jokes about a particular group of people or a profession. So you have jokes about lawyers or teachers and so on. Usually the jokes make fun of the group in some way.

Host: I see. . . .

Sanders: Now, you have to be careful when you tell this type of joke because many people find them offensive, especially if they're about an ethnic or religious group.

Host: But I noticed that Joan told us she's a lawyer before she told the joke. Isn't it sometimes O.K. to tell a joke about a group you belong to?

Sanders: Yes, that's true. People often make jokes about their own group as a way of showing group solidarity, or just to make fun of themselves. But the same jokes are offensive when they are told by someone outside the group.

Host: I see. O.K., let's go to another call.

LISTENING FOR DETAILS

(Repeat Listening for Main Ideas)

REACTING TO THE LISTENING

Exercise 1

Excerpt 1

Host: Now, I have to laugh. You study jokes? That's not really a serious area of study, is it?

Sanders: Oh, but I take my work very seriously.

Excerpt 2

Host: How so?

Sanders: People enjoy the feeling of laughter. It feels good and we like to make other people laugh.

Excerpt 3

Host: So you're going to tell us a lawyer joke?

Joan: Right. Because I know, everyone loves lawyers.

Excerpt 4

Andrew: Because their horns don't work.

Host: Great one, Andrew. Thanks for calling.

B. LISTENING TWO: *More Jokes*

Joke 1

Man: Knock knock.

Woman: Who's there?

Man: Tank.

Woman: Tank who?

Man: You're welcome!

Joke 2

Woman: What do you call an honest lawyer?

Man: Impossible!

Joke 3

Woman: How many government workers does it take to change a light bulb?

Man: I don't know.

Woman: Forty-five. One to change the bulb and forty-four to do the paperwork.

Joke 4

Man: What's as big as an elephant but doesn't weigh anything?

Woman: An elephant's shadow.

Joke 5

Woman: How many tourists does it take to change a light bulb?

Man: I give up.

Woman: Six. One to change the bulb and five to ask for directions.

Joke 6

Woman: Knock knock.

Man: Who's there?

Woman: Avenue.

Man: Avenue who?

Woman: Avenue heard this joke before?

Joke 7

Man: What's black and white and green and black and white and green?

Woman: A zebra rolling down a hill with a leaf in its mouth.

Joke 8

Woman: What do you get when you cross an encyclopedia with a lawyer?

Man: All the information you need—but you can't understand a word of it.

C. LINKING LISTENINGS ONE AND TWO

Exercise 1

(Repeat Listening Two)

A. PRONUNCIATION: *Reduction of* h *in pronouns*

What's his name?

What did he do?

Exercise 1

1. Where did he go?

2. What's her name?

3. I heard his jokes.

4. They made fun of him.

5. He told her a riddle.

Exercise 2

1. Knock knock.

   Who's there?

   Izzy.

   Izzy who?

   Izzy home?

2. Knock knock.

   Who's there?

   Teller.

   Teller who?

   Teller I'm here.

3. Knock knock.

   Who's there?

   Callim.

   Callim who?

   Callim today.

4. Knock knock.

   Who's there?

   Writer.

   Writer who?

   Writer a letter.

5. Knock, knock.

   Who's there?

   Tellis.

   Tellis who?

   Tellis mother to come.

UNIT 8: Traditional or Trendy?

A. LISTENING ONE: *Interview with Shanika De Silva*

Announcer: Today we continue our series "Traditional Dress throughout the World." Our journey takes us to Sri Lanka. Shanika De Silva, a native Sri Lankan now living in Los Angeles, California, shares her thoughts on traditional dress in her home country.

LISTENING FOR MAIN IDEAS

Announcer: Today we continue our series, "Traditional Dress throughout the World." Our journey takes us to Sri Lanka. Shanika De Silva, a native Sri Lankan now living in Los Angeles, California, shares her thoughts on traditional dress in her home country.

Interviewer: Shanika, thanks for joining us today.

Shanika: My pleasure.

Interviewer: First of all, I'd like to ask you . . . what's the traditional clothing in Sri Lanka?

Shanika: Well, for women it's a sari. It's a long piece of cloth that's wrapped around your waist. And then it goes over your shoulder.

Interviewer: And do most women in Sri Lanka wear saris?

Shanika: Most of the older women wear a sari every day. The younger women tend to wear dresses or pants or something.

Interviewer: Why don't the younger women wear saris?

Shanika: Well, I guess some of them feel that the saris are hot and difficult to walk in . . . because they're long.

Interviewer: Sounds like saris aren't very practical.

Shanika: Some people feel that way. Also, many younger women think saris are old-fashioned. They're great for formal occasions, but if you're hanging out with friends, you want something more modern.

Interviewer: So younger women want to be more modern.

Shanika: Actually, I shouldn't say all younger women. It depends on your family history. You see . . . there are two main groups of people in Sri Lanka—the Sinhalese and the Tamils. Then there are some other ethnic groups, like the Sri Lankans, who are part European. The women who are part European tend to wear Western clothing because . . . well, they had relatives who wore Western clothing. But the women who are Sinhalese or Tamil tend to be more traditional.

Interviewer: Because they didn't have that Western influence?

Shanika: Right!

Interviewer: So you're saying that family background can influence the way you dress.

Shanika: Yes, I think it does.

Interviewer: We've been talking about what women wear. How about men? Do they have traditional clothing?

Shanika: The men, I guess, used to wear a sarong. It's this long piece of cloth that's wrapped around the waist.

Interviewer: You say "used to." . . . Don't they wear them anymore?

Shanika: People who live in the countryside still wear sarongs. But in the city, men wear pants and shirts. They only wear sarongs to relax at home.

Interviewer: Interesting! . . . Can I switch gears and ask you a personal question?

Shanika: Sure!

Interviewer: Is traditional clothing important to you?

Shanika: It's funny, because when I was a kid growing up in Sri Lanka, I didn't want to wear saris. But now that I'm older, I like to wear them sometimes. Like my wedding . . . I wore a white sari for my wedding.

Interviewer: Why has your attitude changed, do you think?

Shanika: I guess when you're older you can see the value in it more. When you're younger, you're more interested in being in style . . . you know . . . wearing Levi's and stuff like that. Now I think about saris as something unique from my culture. It's nice to have something different to wear, and in the U.S., a sari is really exotic.

Interviewer: It certainly is! Well, unfortunately, our time's up. Thanks for talking with us, Shanika.

Shanika: You're welcome!

LISTENING FOR DETAILS

(Repeat Listening for Main Ideas)

REACTING TO THE LISTENING

Exercise 1

Excerpt 1

Interviewer: Why don't the younger women wear saris?

Shanika: Well, I guess some of them feel that the saris are hot and difficult to walk in . . . because they're long.

Excerpt 2

Interviewer: Sounds like saris aren't very practical.

Shanika: Some people feel that way. Also, many younger women think saris are old-fashioned. They're great for formal occasions, but if you're hanging out with friends, you want something more modern.

Excerpt 3

Interviewer: Is traditional clothing important to you?

Shanika: It's funny, because when I was a kid growing up in Sri Lanka, I didn't want to wear saris. But now that I'm older, I like to wear them sometimes. Like my wedding . . . I wore a white sari for my wedding.

Excerpt 4

Interviewer: Why has your attitude changed, do you think?

Shanika: I guess when you're older you can see the value in it more. When you're younger, you're more interested in being in style . . . you know . . . wearing Levi's and stuff like that. Now I think about saris as something unique from my culture. It's nice to have something different to wear, and in the U.S., a sari is really exotic.

B. LISTENING TWO: *Interview with a Fashion Designer*

Exercise 2

Reporter: This is Sandra Day in New York reporting on "The World of Work" fashion show. Designer Marco Bellini is with me. Marco, thanks for joining us!

Marco: My pleasure!

Reporter: Could you tell us about today's show?

Marco: Well, Sandra, today we'll be seeing the latest styles in men's casual clothing for the workplace.

Reporter: I've heard about this casual trend. Are a lot of businesses doing it?

Marco: Oh, yes. About half of the big companies are allowing employees to dress down, as they say. Some do it once a week or just in the summer. Others do it every day.

Reporter: What's a typical outfit in a casual office?

Marco: Comfort is important, but you need to look stylish. No old or torn clothes. No messy hair. You might wear a sweater instead of a jacket and tie. And polo shirts with light brown pants are popular. The colors tend to be soft, not flashy or bright.

Reporter: Now this move to casual . . . has it affected business?

Marco: Actually, business has improved. Companies are finding that if their employees are comfortable, they work longer hours. Also, they don't have to spend so much on clothes, so it's like getting a salary raise. That makes people want to work for you.

Reporter: What about supervisors? Are they going casual too?

Marco: Some are. Some people complain that nowadays it's hard to tell the difference between a worker and a supervisor. But most employees like that. It makes everyone feel more equal.

Reporter: O.K. . . . Looks like the fashion show's starting. . . . And here we have our first outfit . . .

A. PRONUNCIATION: *Thought Groups*

Exercise 1

1. It's a long piece of cloth that's wrapped around your waist.

2. They're great for formal occasions, but if you're hanging out with friends, you want something more modern.

3. . . . family background can influence the way you dress.

4. The men, I guess, used to wear a sarong.

5. . . . when I was a kid growing up in Sri Lanka, I didn't want to wear saris.

6. But now that I'm older, I like to wear saris sometimes.

UNIT 9: To Spank or Not to Spank?

A. LISTENING ONE: *A Radio Report*

Announcer: A father was recently arrested by the police for spanking his child, starting a debate among the American public about spanking. Is spanking, or other types of corporal punishment, an acceptable form of discipline for children? Or is it a form of child abuse?

LISTENING FOR MAIN IDEAS

Announcer: A father was recently arrested by the police for spanking his child, starting a debate among the American public about spanking. Is spanking, or other types of corporal punishment, an acceptable form of discipline for children? Or is it a form of child abuse? Charles Dean has our report.

Reporter: The case that has everyone talking is the arrest of Dale Clover, a thirty-six-year-old father of three, at a shopping mall in St. Louis, Missouri. He was arrested after an employee at the mall saw him spanking his five-year-old son, Donny, and called the police. The father was arrested for child abuse. Mr. Clover admits that he hit his son but says that it wasn't child abuse. He says it was discipline. Across the country, parents disagree on this issue: What is the difference between loving discipline and child abuse? Some parents, like Rhonda Moore, see a clear difference between spanking and child abuse.

Rhonda Moore: A little bit of pain is necessary to teach a child what is right and wrong. It's like burning your hand when you touch a hot stove. Pain is nature's way of teaching us. Spanking is done out of love. Child abuse is done out of anger, when the parent loses control. When I spank my children, I always talk to them before and afterward, and explain why they are being spanked. I explain what they did wrong, and they remember not to do it again. They respect me as a parent. My children understand that I'm spanking them for their own good.

Reporter: Taylor Robinson, father of four, feels that parents should never hit their children for any reason.

Taylor Robinson: I want my children to learn right and wrong, but not out of fear of being hit. Spanking teaches children to fear their parents, not respect them. When a parent spanks a child, what the child learns is that problems should be solved with violence. They learn that it's acceptable for parents to hurt their children. None of these are lessons that I want to teach my children. I want my children to learn to talk about their problems and solve them without violence, but spanking doesn't teach that.

Reporter: Parents are split about corporal punishment, and doctors also disagree about the issue. Dr. John Oparah thinks our child abuse laws sometimes go too far.

Dr. John Oparah: Today, many children don't respect their parents. Children need strong, loving discipline. Sometimes spanking is the best way to get a child's attention, to make sure the child listens to the parent. I've known loving parents who have had police officers come to their door and say, "Your child reported that you hit him." They're treated like criminals. As a society, we complain all the time that our young people are getting into more and more trouble, committing crimes—yet when parents try to control their children, they're punished. Some parents are afraid to discipline their children because their neighbors might call the police.

Reporter: However, most doctors say that there are many harmful effects of spanking. Dr. Beverly Lau is opposed to spanking.

Dr. Beverly Lau: Spanking can lead to more violent behavior in children. Studies show that children who are spanked are more violent when they grow up. In the long run, spanking doesn't work well; it's not as effective as other forms of discipline. A child may stop misbehaving for the moment, but over time, children who are spanked actually misbehave more than children who are not spanked. Research shows that if you want a peaceful family, don't spank your kids.

Reporter: The issue of spanking and corporal punishment will continue to be debated among parents and in the courts. In Dale Clover's case, he could get up to five years in prison if he is convicted of child abuse.

LISTENING FOR DETAILS

(Repeat Listening for Main Ideas)

REACTING TO THE LISTENING

Exercise 1

Excerpt 1

Rhonda Moore: Spanking is done out of love. Child abuse is done out of anger, when the parent loses control. When I spank my children, I always talk to them before and afterward, and explain why they are being spanked.

Excerpt 2

Taylor Robinson: When a parent spanks a child, what the child learns is that problems should be solved with violence. They learn that it's acceptable for parents to hurt their children. None of these are lessons that I want to teach my children.

Excerpt 3

Dr. John Oparah: Today, many children don't respect their parents. Children need strong, loving discipline. Sometimes spanking is the best way to get a child's attention, to make sure the child listens to the parent.

Excerpt 4

Dr. Beverly Lau: In the long run, spanking doesn't work well; it's not as effective as other forms of discipline. A child may stop misbehaving for the moment, but over time, children who are spanked actually misbehave more than children who are not spanked.

B. LISTENING TWO: *Expert Opinions*

Announcer: What are the long-term effects of spanking as a child gets older and becomes an adult? Listen to the opinions of three experts. Donald Sterling, a lawyer and psychologist who interviews criminals before they go to trial . . .

Sterling: I've seen it over and over again. Violent criminals were almost always spanked and hit when they were children. This corporal punishment teaches children to be violent when they are very young, so when they are adults, they commit crimes and abuse their wives and children. And then their children grow up to be violent, and the cycle continues.

Announcer: Dr. Phyllis Jones from the Center for Family Research.

Jones: We studied 332 families to see how parents' actions affected teenagers' behavior. We found that teenagers did better when they had clear discipline as a child. Some of these parents used spanking as a form of discipline, and some didn't. It seems that spanking doesn't hurt children if it's done in a loving home, but it's most important to talk to your children and spend time with them. Spanking should be the choice of the parents.

Announcer: Lois Goldin, child psychologist.

Goldin: In the United States, the number of parents who spank their kids is decreasing, and people who oppose spanking say that's good because it will make our society less violent. But look at the statistics. Actually, violent crime is rising every year, and the number of teenagers and children that commit crimes is going up the fastest! Parents need to control their children better, and corporal punishment is one way to do that.

PRONUNCIATION: *Final Consonants*

Exercise 1

1. He asked the counselor to <u>advise</u> him.

2. The counselor gave him some <u>advice</u>.

Exercise 3

abuse	abuse	rise	rice
lose	loose	plays	place
peas	peace	knees	niece
eyes	ice	advise	advice
fears	fierce	raise	race

Exercise 4

abuse	rice
lose	plays
peace	niece
ice	advise
fears	race

Exercise 6

1. The advisor gave them some advice to raise race horses.
2. Did the police abuse Dale Clover's rights when they arrested him for child abuse?
3. My niece hurt her knees, so I placed some frozen peas on them.
4. My son fears that our neighbor's fierce dog will lose his collar and get loose.

UNIT 10: Before You Say "I Do"

A. LISTENING ONE: *A Prenuptial Agreement*

Reporter: When most couples marry, they may discuss some things in advance, like how many children they want or where they want to live, but most of the day-to-day details and problems of married life are worked out after marriage. Not so with Steve and Karen Parsons, who have a fifteen-page prenuptial agreement that states the rules they must follow in almost every aspect of their married life.

LISTENING FOR MAIN IDEAS

Reporter: When most couples marry, they may discuss some things in advance, like how many children they want or where they want to live, but most of the day-to-day details and problems of married life are worked out after marriage. Not so with Steve and Karen Parsons, who have a fifteen-page prenuptial agreement that states the rules they must follow in almost every aspect of their married life.

Steve, Karen, first I'd like to ask you why you decided to write this agreement. You've both been married before, am I right?

Steve: Yes. I've been married twice, and Karen was married once before.

Karen: So we have some experience about what goes wrong in a marriage.

Reporter: And that's why you wrote this agreement?

Steve: Yes, we found that many problems happen when a person has different expectations from his or her spouse. We wanted to talk about everything openly and honestly before we started living together.

Karen: Also, we both know how important it is to respect each other's quirks. We're all bothered by things that seem small to someone else. Like, it used to really bother me when my ex-husband left his dirty clothes on the floor, so we put that in the agreement: "Dirty clothing must be put in the laundry bag." Now Steve knows what my expectations are.

Reporter: I'm sure that some people hearing this report will think that this contract isn't very romantic.

Steve: Well, we disagree.

Karen: We think it's very romantic.

Steve: This contract shows that we sat down and talked and really tried to understand the other person. A lot of problems occur in a marriage because people don't talk about what they want.

Karen: That's right! When we disagree about something, we work out a compromise that's good for both of us. I'd much rather do that than get some "romantic" gift like flowers or candy.

Reporter: Some of these rules sound like . . . sound like, well, a business agreement. Many of your rules concern money in some way. . . even the rules about having children.

Karen: In our experience, disagreements about money can cause a lot of problems, so we talked about how we want to spend our money and put that in the agreement as well.

Reporter: So, do you spend a lot of time checking on each other to see if the rules are being followed?

Karen: No, not at all. And we don't argue about them, either.

Steve: As a matter of fact, I think we spend less time arguing than most couples because we both know what the other person expects.

Karen: Yeah, we can spend our time doing things we enjoy and just being with each other.

Reporter: What happens if one of you breaks a rule?

Steve: We don't think that will be a problem. . . .

Karen: No.

Steve: Because we've agreed on these rules.

Reporter: But what if, say, you don't . . . don't want to cook dinner one night? What happens?

Steve: Well, we'll talk about it and reach a compromise. Maybe there's a good reason.

Reporter: But if you break a lot of rules, all the time . . .

Karen: Then we have to ask: Is this marriage really working? Because if we can't follow our own agreement, there's no point.

Reporter: So it sounds like you two are happy with this agreement. Do you think other couples should follow your example, and write prenuptial agreements of their own?

Steve: It's a lot of work to write an agreement, but I think it could be useful to a lot of people.

Karen: Maybe there would be fewer divorces if everyone did this.

LISTENING FOR DETAILS

(Repeat Listening for Main Ideas)

REACTING TO THE LISTENING

Exercise 1

Excerpt 1

Steve: Yes, we found that many problems happen when a person has different expectations from his or her spouse. We wanted to talk about everything openly and honestly before we started living together.

Karen: Also, we both know how important it is to respect each other's quirks. We're all bothered by things that seem small to someone else. Like, it used to really bother me when my ex-husband left his dirty clothes on the floor, so we put that in the agreement: "Dirty clothing must be put in the laundry bag." Now Steve knows what my expectations are.

Excerpt 2

Reporter: I'm sure that some people hearing this report will think that this contract isn't very romantic.

Steve: Well, we disagree.

Karen: We think it's very romantic.

Steve: This contract shows that we sat down and talked and really tried to understand the other person. A lot of problems occur in a marriage because people don't talk about what they want.

Karen: That's right! When we disagree about something, we work out a compromise that's good for both of us. I'd much rather do that than get some "romantic" gift like flowers or candy.

Excerpt 3

Reporter: So, do you spend a lot of time checking on each other to see if the rules are being followed?

Karen: No, not at all. And we don't argue about them, either.

Steve: As a matter of fact, I think we spend less time arguing than most couples because we both know what the other person expects.

Karen: Yeah, we can spend our time doing things we enjoy and just being with each other.

Reporter: What happens if one of you breaks a rule?

Steve: We don't think that will be a problem.

Karen: No.

Steve: Because we've agreed on these rules.

B. LISTENING TWO: *Reactions to the Prenuptial Agreement*

Speaker 1: This contract? No way. I would never do this. It's not very romantic. I think that if you really love someone, you don't need to write all these things down. You just learn how to make your spouse happy and talk about problems when they come up.

Speaker 2: It might be a good idea, but I think this contract has too many details. For example, the rule about going to sleep at 11:00 P.M. What if one spouse wasn't sleepy or wanted to watch the news? That would be breaking a rule. It's crazy. You can't plan every detail in your life.

Speaker 3: I think it's a great idea! I bet there would be a lot fewer divorces if everyone did this. Most couples don't know how to talk about their problems. They let small things bother them until they finally blow up. Then they fight, but they don't know how to say "I'm sorry" afterwards. A contract like this would teach couples how to talk about their problems.

Speaker 4: I'm a lawyer, and I can tell you that this isn't a legal contract. What I mean is, if you go to court and say, "I want a divorce because my wife didn't eat healthy food," well, the judge wouldn't give you a divorce for that reason. So, legally, this contract has no power.

Speaker 5: I think the contract could be useful to help couples decide if they really should get married. A lot of couples get married because of their romantic feelings for the other person, but they don't look carefully at who the person is. I think this contract would make both people think carefully about whether they should get married.

A. PRONUNCIATION: *Contrastive Stress*

Exercise 1

1. Karen will do the grocery shopping.
2. Karen will always use a shopping list.
3. Nothing will be left on the floor in the bedroom.
4. On weekdays, we will go to bed at 11:00.
5. We will wait three years before buying a house.
6. Karen will make a list of groceries every week.
7. We will spend at least 15 minutes a day talking with each other.
8. Steve will figure out directions before we start a trip.
9. We will eat healthy food that's low in fat and sugar.
10. We will update this agreement every year.

The Phonetic Alphabet

Consonant Symbols

/b/	be		/t/	to
/d/	do		/v/	van
/f/	father		/w/	will
/g/	get		/y/	yes
/h/	he		/z/	zoo, busy
/k/	keep, can		/θ/	thanks
/l/	let		/ð/	then
/m/	may		/ʃ/	she
/n/	no		/ʒ/	vision, Asia
/p/	pen		/tʃ/	child
/r/	rain		/dʒ/	join
/s/	so, circle		/ŋ/	long

Vowel Symbols

/ɑ/	far, hot		/iy/	we, mean, feet
/ɛ/	met, said		/ey/	day, late, rain
/ɔ/	tall, bought		/ow/	go, low, coat
/ə/	son, under		/uw/	too, blue
/æ/	cat		/ay/	time, buy
/ɪ/	ship		/aw/	house, now
/ʊ/	good, could, put		/oy/	boy, coin

Credits

Photo credits: Page 1 (left) Ron Case/Getty Images, (right) Spike Mafford/Getty Images; **Page 10** (top) Pete Seaward/Getty Images, (bottom left and right) Barros & Barros/Getty Images; **Page 19** John Terence Turner/Getty Images; **Pages 37, 40** www.freeimages.co.uk; **Page 55** Spencer Grant/PhotoEdit; **Page 57** Photograph by Michael Pateman; **Pages 91, 93** Karen Su/Corbis; **Page 123** David Turnley/Corbis; **Page 127** Courtesy of David Schmidt; **Page 163** Andy Marcus/Digital Vision Ltd.

Text art: Lloyd P. Birmingham, pages 22, 28, 128, 141, 153; John Dyess, pages 59, 64; Paul McCusker, pages 21, 44, 76, 132; Dusan Petricic, pages 73, 109, 110, 111, 112, 145.

Listening selections and text credits: Page 57 Adapted from "Jackie Tales: The Magic of Creating Stories and the Art of Telling Them" by Jackie Torrence (New York: Avon Books, Inc., 1998); **Page 59** Audio program that accompanies this text courtesy of Rounder Records Corp., One Camp Street, Cambridge, Massachusetts 02140 U.S.A.; **Page 62** From "Storytelling Torrence Describes Her Craft." © Copyright NPR® 1998. The text and audio of a news interview by NPR's Frank Stasio was originally broadcast on National Public Radio's "Weekend Edition® Sunday" on June 28, 1998, and is used with the permission of National Public Radio, Inc. Any unauthorized duplication is strictly prohibited.

Reviewers

Lubie G. Alatriste, Lehman College; A. Morgan Andaluz, Leeward Community College; Chris Antonellis, Boston University CELOP; Christine Baez, Universidad de las Américas, Mexico City, Mexico; Betty Baron, Johnson County Community College; Rudy Besikof, University of California San Diego; Mary Black, Institute of North American Studies; Dorothy Buroh, University of California, San Diego; Kay Caldwell, Leeward Community College; Margarita Canales; Universidad Latinoamericana, Mexico City, Mexico; Jose Carvalho, University of Massachusetts Boston; Philip R. Condorelli, University of Massachusetts Boston; Pamela Couch, Boston University CELOP; Barbara F. Dingee, University of Massachusetts Boston; Jeanne M. Dunnet, Central Connecticut State University; Samuela Eckstut-Didier, Boston University CELOP; Patricia Hedden, Yonsei University; Hostos Community College; GEOS Language Institute; Jennifer M. Gerrity, University of Massachusetts Boston; Lis Jenkinson, Northern Virginia Community College; Glenna Jennings, University of California, San Diego; Diana Jones, Instituto Angloamericano, Mexico City, Mexico; Matt Kaeiser, Old Dominion University; Regina Kandraska, University of Massachusetts Boston; King Fahd University of Petroleum & Minerals; Chris Ko, Kyang Hee University; Charalambos Kollias, The Hellenic-American Union; Barbara Kruchin, Columbia University ALP; Language Training Institute; Jacqueline LoConde, Boston University CELOP; Mary Lynch, University of Massachusetts Boston; Julia Paranionova, Moscow State Pedagogical University; Pasadena City College; Pontifical Xavier University; Natalya Morozova, Moscow State Pedagogical University; Mary Carole Ramiowski, University of Seoul; Jon Robinson, University of Seoul; Michael Sagliano, Leeward Community College; Janet Shanks, Columbia University ALP; Eric Tejeda; PROULEX, Guadalajara, Mexico; Truman College; United Arab Emirates University; University of Minnesota; Karen Whitlow, Johnson County Community College

Notes